THE WAY OF KINSHIP
THE ART OF LIVING FROM THE DAODEJING
(TAO TE CHING)

JIM JONES

Published by Jim Jones

www.Kinship.Cafe

ISBN:

979-8-9932462-1-5 Hardcover

979-8-9932462-0-8 Paperback

979-8-9932462-2-2 Ebook

Dedicated to my fellow travelers on the Way.

CONTENTS

A NOTE ON THE TRANSLATION

Any passage of the Daodejing that is not attributed to a specific author is my translation, reflecting over a decade of dedicated study of the text from a philosophical naturalist perspective. Although I am not formally trained as a scholar of Classical Chinese, my work has been deeply informed by careful engagement with the original language through academic resources, including the writings of Classical Chinese scholars and language study applications.

My focus in translating the Daodejing is on its social and personal implications — how its ideas can illuminate ways of living and relating within the natural world and human society. Rather than aiming for a strictly linguistic or doctrinal rendering, I have sought to strike a balance between fidelity to the original text and philosophical clarity, offering a reading that invites reflection on the Daodejing's enduring relevance to contemporary life.

Where the original text is ambiguous — as it often is — I have leaned toward interpretations that highlight naturalistic, relational, and emergent aspects of existence, staying close to the spirit of the work as a guide. In doing so,

I have drawn on the insights of recognized scholars while allowing my engagement with the text to shape the final form of the translation.

I encourage readers to view my translations not as a definitive or "authoritative" version but as one possible lens through which the profound and elusive vision of the Daodejing might be encountered.

A NOTE ON SPELLING

One of the first things you may notice when approaching the Daodejing (道德經) is that it appears under different spellings — sometimes as Tao Te Ching, other times as Daodejing; its author as Lao Tzu or Laozi (老子). These differences arise from two major systems used to Romanize Chinese characters. The older system, Wade-Giles, was widely used in Western scholarship until the mid-20th century and spells the title as Tao Te Ching and the author's name as Lao Tzu. The newer system, Pinyin, was adopted in the People's Republic of China in the 1950s and is now the international standard. It renders the same terms as Daodejing and Laozi. Though they look quite different in English, the underlying Chinese sounds remain the same. Whether one spells it Tao Te Ching and Lao Tzu or Daodejing and Laozi, they are pronounced the same way: Dow-duh-jing and Lao-dzuh.

INTRODUCTION: THE WAY OF KINSHIP

What if belonging isn't something we earn, but something we remember? This book is about remembering what the modern world taught us to forget — that we are already connected, already held in a web of mutual becoming. We recover this memory as we walk through life in light of an ancient perspective — oneness. I was reminded of this while studying the Daodejing.

A 2,500-year-old tiny book of Chinese philosophy might sound like odd reading material for a 21st-century American software engineer. I was on a quest to find my place in the world and what I should do with my life. Never feeling like I fit in motivated me to find out where I belong and what my life is all about. For decades, I studied religion, science, and philosophy, including the Daodejing, looking for answers. My studies led me to view the world through the lens of Philosophical Naturalism, a scientific worldview that posits the natural world as the sole existence. Intellectually, Philosophical Naturalism is very satisfying, but it does not come with a personal code, a direction, a way of life. In the Daodejing, I found an ancient naturalistic philosophy presented as a way of life. With these two philosophical perspectives, I discovered a sense of belonging.

The Way of Kinship is my phrase to describe this way of life shaped by the wisdom of the Daodejing and the insights of Philosophical Naturalism. Kinship is not a word we often use these days. It is most commonly understood as the network of relationships that connect people through blood, marriage, or shared lineage. The Way of Kinship invites us to a broader and more essential understanding, to a felt experience of relatedness — a recognition that one's existence is intertwined with the lives of others. It extends beyond legal or biological ties to include bonds of affection, responsibility, and shared fate. It is in this deeper sense that I am using the word. The Way of Kinship is not merely a social structure but a way of perceiving the world.

To live the Way of Kinship is to see the self not as separate but as embedded within a web of mutual influence and care — with other humans, with animals, with ecosystems, and with the processes that sustain life. It is to recognize that one's well-being is inseparable from the well-being of others. In many Indigenous and ecological worldviews, kinship extends to the land, rivers, weather, and stars, affirming that the world is not full of objects but relations. This expanded sense of kinship challenges the boundaries drawn by modern individualism and invites a return to a more integrated way of belonging — one grounded not in ownership or control but in reverence, reciprocity, and shared becoming.

I have embraced this path. In our world, it is difficult to follow the Way of Kinship. We are pulled in the opposite direction — toward isolation, competition, control, and speed. The systems we live in reward disconnection from nature, from others, and even from ourselves. Politics has become divisive to the point of zero compromise. The horrors of war continue to plague our world. Economics has become inextricably linked to environmental degradation and the exploitation of labor. The constant struggle for survival leaves so many of us bereft of community and rejuvenation.

While our problems are real and present, they are not new. The Daodejing was written in a time of similar turmoil, during the Warring States period (475-221 BCE), when violence, corruption, and rigid hierarchies fractured every level of society. Its verses speak directly to the consequences of overreach, domination, and disconnection from the natural order. It does not offer policy solutions or utopian dreams but something more profound: a call to reorient ourselves toward a different way of living — one grounded in humility, balance, and harmony with the unfolding patterns of life. The issues we face today may wear modern masks, but the Daodejing sees through to the enduring roots of human imbalance — and gently points us toward a wiser, more integrated path.

To walk the Way of Kinship is to resist the illusion of separateness and cultivate a deep sense of belonging. It is not an easy path but a profoundly human one — a return to what has always connected us, though we may have forgotten: that we are not alone and never were.

HOW THIS BOOK CAN CHANGE YOUR LIFE

Reading a book can change your life by altering your perspective on the world; perception shapes everything. We don't encounter reality as it is; we encounter it through the lens of our understanding — through the stories we believe, the categories we rely on, and the patterns we recognize. A truly powerful book introduces new lenses. It names what we've felt but couldn't express. It shows us relationships we hadn't noticed. It challenges assumptions we didn't even know we were making. When a book shifts your perception, the world appears different — not because the facts have changed, but because your orientation to them has. What once seemed inevitable might now appear constructed. What once felt separate might now feel connected. This shift in perception can lead to new choices, new values, and even a new sense of self. In this way, reading is not just intellectual; it is transformational — a quiet act that can profoundly reconfigure how you live.

Here is the central thesis of this book: Perception shapes experience, and experience shapes action. How we see the world sets the course for how we live. When we adopt the perception I call the Way of Kinship, we begin to cultivate experiences and actions that lead to a richer, more dynamic life and a vital future for those who come after us.

The philosophy of the Daodejing serves as a powerful guide on this journey, a companion in reawakening our deepest sense of belonging and alignment with the living world.

I have structured this book to help present a transformative understanding of the Way of Kinship and the underlying concepts from Philosophical Naturalism and the Daodejing. The introduction will continue with further orientation of our relationship with the world and some background on the Daodejing.

Part One addresses the core perspective of oneness. Oneness is the largest topic as it is the foundation on which the rest of the book depends. After exploring oneness from several different angles, I will turn to chapter one of the Daodejing and provide an in-depth commentary on its unique take on oneness.

Part Two shifts to addressing how the perspective of oneness shapes our actions and our view of ourselves. This part contains an in-depth commentary on chapter thirty-eight of the Daodejing for its unique take on how oneness is manifested in our actions. The balance of Part Two covers several topics related to everyday living and offers several suggestions on how to practice or incorporate these ideas into your life.

Now that you know where we are going, let's return to the introduction and look at how our subjective experience of life works.

SUBJECTIVE EXPERIENCE

Take this common situation as an example. You are driving down the freeway, and out of the blue, a car cuts in front of you, so close that you must put on the brakes. You honk your horn and yell a few choice expletives at the other car. To analyze this situation, we need to break it down into its parts. Let's start by modeling the situation. We will call the car cutting you off the Stimulus, and you're honking and yelling the Response. We can then model the process as follows:

Stimulus $\rightarrow$ Response

A surface-level reflection leads one to think that the Stimulus caused the Response. In this case, the strategy for avoiding honking and yelling at other cars is for them not to cut you off. There is nothing you can do in this situation; only the other driver can change it. While you hold to this model of the situation, if someone in the car with you suggests that you shouldn't honk and yell, you might receive the comment as asking you to ignore the wrong thing that someone else did or that you should try to suppress what you rightfully feel. And this reveals a key point: you are acting as a result of how you feel. We should update our model of the situation:

.   .   .

Stimulus → Emotion → Response

Now we see that the Stimulus is causing an Emotion, and the Emotion is causing the Response. If we return to the example situation, the car cutting you off makes you angry, and your anger results in you honking and yelling. Suppose your annoying passenger again suggests you shouldn't honk and yell. In that case, it comes across as implying that your feelings are not valid and that somehow you are wrong for feeling angry when the car cut you off.

But let's assume that you have come to the conclusion that you shouldn't be honking and yelling. You don't like how it sets you off for the rest of the day, or you're concerned that your blood pressure is getting too high. Yet you feel what you feel. What can you do? There is a missing non-obvious piece of our model. While it may seem that the Stimulus causes an Emotion, there is another step. Here is the final model:

Stimulus → Perception → Emotion → Response

How we Perceive (or interpret) the Stimulus is what causes the Emotion that drives the Response. Let's review how the initial example looks when we apply the complete model. You are driving down the freeway, and out of the blue, a car cuts in front of you, so close that you must put on the brakes. You unconsciously assume that the other driver is a jerk who doesn't care about safety on the road. This assumption about the driver makes you angry and maybe a bit scared, so you honk your horn and yell a few choice expletives at the other car.

The complete model helps us to see what we need to do. If you don't want to be angry, so you don't honk and yell, then you need to address how you perceive the situation of the car cutting you off. The truth is that you don't actually know anything about why the car cut you off. Perhaps you were in their blind spot, and they innocently didn't see you. Has that ever happened to you? What if they just found out their son was in an accident, and they were rushing to the hospital?

My daughter's friend, Vivian, shared an alternative way of perceiving the same situation. When she gets cut off in traffic, she thinks to herself, "Man, they must really have to go poo." If this were your default assumption about why the other car cut you off, rather than being angry, you might even wish them God's speed!

If it rubs you the wrong way to assume this made-up story about the other driver, remember that the story you told yourself about the driver that made you angry is also made-up. The fact is that we have no idea what is in the other driver's mind. The point we are concerned with is how we respond to the situation. A response in which we do not get angry or upset at the situation. The story (or perception) through which we view the situation will elicit a different emotional response. Swapping out which story we interpret the situation through is also called reframing the situation.

For this reframing of the situation in a new story to

work, you must intentionally catch yourself when you notice that you are starting to get angry at being cut off. At that point, you remind yourself of the new story and that you don't know it to be otherwise. If you do this enough, you will eventually not need to catch yourself; it will become your new default response to that type of situation, and you will no longer get angry at other drivers!

Learning to tell yourself a new default story when getting cut off in traffic is a basic example. Still, it helps to illustrate that our perception of a situation dictates our emotional experience of the situation, which leads to our response. Our goal with this book is to replace our foundational story through which we see the world with the story of the Way of Kinship. Let's look a little deeper into the core concept of the Way of Kinship: interconnectedness.

KINSHIP WITH THE WORLD

At the human level, no one exists in isolation. From the moment of birth, we are dependent on others, not just biologically, in the sense that we come from other people, but emotionally and developmentally. We rely on caregivers to survive infancy, to teach language, and to help us form our first ideas about the world. As we grow, our sense of identity, purpose, and even health is shaped by our relationships with others. Humans are profoundly social creatures, and our flourishing is inseparable from the presence and support of other people.

Beyond interpersonal dependence, we are also fundamentally reliant on the natural world. Air, water, shelter, and food are the basic requirements for human life, and each depends on complex ecological systems. These systems involve plants, animals, microorganisms, climate patterns, and geological structures. For example, the oxygen we breathe is the byproduct of photosynthesis, which plants and algae perform. Our food comes from soil enriched by decaying matter, water cycles powered by evaporation and rain, and pollinators like bees. None of these elements could exist in isolation; they are sustained by delicate balances and interactions across the biosphere.

Broadening our view, we see that ecological systems are possible only because of the formation of the planet and the presence of a stable sun. Earth's distance from the sun, magnetic field, and atmosphere are all products of astronomical processes that unfolded over billions of years. Like all stars, the sun results from earlier generations of stars that lived, died, and scattered heavier elements into space. These elements formed new solar systems, planets, and, eventually, the conditions for life. The chain of prior interactions reaches back to the Big Bang. This singular origin point generated our universe's fundamental particles and forces.

In this light, every human breath is an echo of cosmic events. To exist is to participate in a vast chain of interdependence, where everything from our relationships to our atoms links us to everything else. This perspective doesn't just highlight our vulnerability and need; it can also foster humility, gratitude, and a sense of belonging within a universe that is not random chaos but deeply interconnected.

Recognizing the deep interconnectedness of all things profoundly alters how we experience life and the kinds of actions we feel compelled to take. When we see ourselves not as isolated individuals but as participants in a vast, interwoven web of existence, our sense of identity and responsibility shift. We begin to understand that our well-being is inseparable from the well-being of others, including people, ecosystems, and the planet as a whole. This awareness can lead to greater empathy because others' suffering is no longer seen as separate from our own. It also fosters a deeper sense of gratitude and humility, knowing that our very existence is made possible by countless processes and beings we did not create and cannot control.

In practical terms, this worldview encourages more cooperative, sustainable, and compassionate behavior. Suppose we recognize that our health is tied to clean air and water. In that case, we become more mindful of how our consumption affects the environment. If we see that our emotional and psychological health depends on relationships, we invest more in community, communication, and care. It becomes harder to justify exploitative economic, environmental, or interpersonal practices when we understand that harming others harms ourselves. Interconnectedness reframes justice from retributive to restorative: a balanced world is one in which life can flourish for all.

This perspective can also alleviate specific existential anxieties. If everything is connected, then even small acts — listening deeply to someone, planting a tree, showing kindness — ripple outward in ways we may never fully see.

Our actions gain meaning beyond immediate outcomes because they are part of a larger whole. Life becomes less about domination or control and more about participation, stewardship, and contribution. In this view, fulfillment arises not from isolation or self-sufficiency but from engagement, reciprocity, and alignment with the greater patterns of life.

Recognizing nature's deep interconnectedness — how everything emerges, transforms, and sustains itself through relationships — invites us to reconsider how we see the world and our place within it. To explore this shift more deeply, we turn to the Daodejing. In its poetic reflections and paradoxical insights, the Daodejing offers a language and a rhythm for understanding the world as a dynamic web of mutual influence. It points us toward a way of seeing and being that flows with the patterns of life.

DISCOVERING THE DAODEJING

My journey to discover the Way of Kinship spans over fifty years. Something in my nature — a mix of temperament, experience, and longing — gave rise to a persistent question: What makes well-being possible, and how do we sustain it? I was born into a nominally Christian home. Since Christianity claimed to hold these answers, it was the natural place to begin my search. I committed fully, earning a Master of Divinity degree and serving as a pastor for fifteen years.

Christianity, however, is not a singular thing. Its manifestations range from the Ku Klux Klan to the Amish, from prosperity gospel preachers to contemplative monks. Trying to make sense of this enormous diversity led me to tools that could help decipher what the biblical authors actually intended. I turned to history, language, cultural anthropology, and social linguistics — all in an effort to hear ancient voices on their own terms.

As I studied how people across time and cultures interpret the world differently, I found myself drawn deeper into the workings of perception itself. How do we form beliefs? What shapes our sense of truth? This led me to the study of the brain, where neuroscience offered insights into cognition, emotion, and the roots of behavior. Yet even here, the questions deepened. To grasp how neurons give rise to thought required venturing into the foundations of matter itself — and so I found myself exploring quantum physics and the strange dance of particles and probabilities that undergirds everything.

Ultimately, these explorations led me beyond the boundaries of Christianity. I no longer felt I could reconcile its theological claims with what I had been learning about the nature of reality, but my quest for well-being remained. That search eventually brought me back to a book I first encountered in the early 1980s: the Daodejing.

The edition was by Feng and English — still one of my favorites — with striking black-and-white nature photography and elegant Chinese calligraphy. Its paradoxical verses and cryptic style intrigued me, even though I could only grasp fragments of its meaning at the time.

Three decades later, that puzzle began to unfold. The tools I had developed in biblical studies helped me re-engage with this ancient Chinese text in a deeper, more respectful way. I approached the Daodejing as a serious work of philosophical insight. What emerged — and continues to emerge through years of study — surprised me.

The Daodejing is not just relevant to personal peace or spiritual balance. It speaks directly to the challenges of our time: ecological collapse, social fragmentation, and political overreach. Its wisdom lies in helping us see more clearly — the patterns of nature, the limits of control, the hidden strength of gentleness, and the quiet power of yielding. It reveals a vision of life grounded in interdependence, humility, and the wisdom of restraint.

Looking back, I see that every step of my journey — from theology to linguistics, from neuroscience to physics — was part of a single unfolding. Each discipline offered a lens, and together, these tools brought me to a place of coherence. The Way of Kinship is not a doctrine I found, but a way of being I've come to recognize — one that aligns with the rhythms of the natural world and the deep structure of relationships at the heart of all things.

A PERSONAL AND SOCIAL PHILOSOPHY BORN IN A TIME OF CHAOS

The origins of the Daodejing are rooted in a time of profound social upheaval. While traditional accounts often focus on the semi-legendary figure of Laozi, the more important context is the turbulent historical backdrop against which the text emerged. The Daodejing was composed during the Warring States period (475-221 BCE) of the Zhou (pronounced Jo) dynasty, a time when China was splintered into numerous rival states, each vying for power through relentless warfare, political intrigue, and shifting alliances. Living through centuries of war is the unspoken background on every page of the Daodejing.

The constant violence and disorder led many thinkers of the time to question the effectiveness of traditional social norms, rituals, and political systems. The older Zhou dynasty's ideals of harmony through hierarchy and ritual had begun to erode, leaving a vacuum that invited philosophical innovation. Against this backdrop, the Daodejing speaks not to the glories of conquest or the strength of rule but to the power of yielding and simplicity. Its emphasis on withdrawing from contention, cultivating inner stillness, and aligning with the natural rhythms of life can be seen as a radical critique of a world obsessed with control and domination.

Moreover, the text reflects the profound disillusionment of an era in which human schemes repeatedly led to ruin. Instead of offering new methods of governance through tradition or moral persuasion (as contemporaries like Confucius did), the Daodejing points toward an alternative path: one that finds strength in softness, success in humility, and clarity in returning to what is essential and unadorned. Its wisdom is shaped not by academic speculation but by lived experience amid the collapse of social order. In this way, the Daodejing carries the silent weight of a world unraveled by war, offering instead a vision of how to live lightly, resiliently, and wisely within it.

A REMEMBERED INDIGENOUS WISDOM

A commercial from the early 1970s had a profound impact on my life. It sounds unbelievable for a commercial to affect someone to that degree. Still, if you were around in those days, you know precisely which commercial I am referring to. The "Crying Indian" Public Service Announcement (PSA) from 1971 opens with a solitary Indian paddling a canoe through a misty, pristine landscape. A vision of our land from long ago. As he moves downstream, the water becomes increasingly choked with trash and pollution. You suddenly realize this is not the past but the present. Eventually, he reaches a shore near a busy highway, where industrial smokestacks loom and motorists carelessly toss garbage onto the roadside. One piece of trash lands at his feet. The camera then zooms in on his face as a single tear falls, accompanied by the solemn voiceover: "Some people have a deep, abiding respect for the natural beauty that was once this country. And some people don't. People start pollution. People can stop it." The PSA closes with an image of the man, silent and grieving, embodying sorrow for what has been lost.

The emotional power of the PSA lies in how it contrasts a remembered Indigenous worldview — one of reverence, integration, and stewardship of the land — with the alienation and casual destruction of the modern industrial world. The Native figure represents a way of being that sees the Earth not as a resource to be consumed but as a living community to which humans belong. His silent grief suggests that this ancient way of life, respectful and harmonious, has been desecrated by modern behaviors fueled by convenience, consumption, and indifference.

This contrast creates a profound moral tension. By invoking an idealized Indigenous perspective, the PSA taps into a deeper cultural memory of what it means to live in balance with nature. This memory stands in stark opposition to contemporary America's polluted highways and smoking factories. It evokes guilt and nostalgia simultaneously, urging viewers to recognize that environmental destruction is not just a technical problem but a spiritual and perceptual failure. The PSA works not only by showing pollution but by quietly mourning the loss of a wiser, older relationship with the Earth — one that modern society must somehow remember or reinvent if it is to heal.

In many ways, Shennong — the mythical "Spiritual Farmer" of early Chinese tradition — serves a role similar to the Crying Indian in understanding the deeper currents beneath the Daodejing. Shennong is remembered as a cultural hero who taught humanity how to cultivate the land, discover medicinal herbs, and live harmoniously with the natural world. He embodies an ancient memory of a time when human life was intimately woven into the rhythms of the Earth, governed not by force or ambition but by observation, patience, and care. In early Chinese thought, Shennong represents a period when society was simple, decentralized, and aligned with the patterns of nature — a golden age before the rise of the dynasties characterized by ambition, warfare, and the drive for power that would define later eras.

In this light, the Daodejing can be understood as a text that mourns the loss of the Shennong-like order and offers a way forward through realignment. Living through the chaos of the Warring States period, its authors and compilers witnessed firsthand the consequences of abandoning natural rhythms for human schemes of domination. Instead of advocating for more laws, punishments, or clever tactics, the Daodejing calls for a return to the Dao: the spontaneous, self-ordering way of nature. It represents not just a philosophy but a cultural memory of a different way of living — a wisdom rooted in simplicity, humility, and non-coercion, offered as a corrective to the violent ambitions tearing their world apart.

A TOOL TO SEE WHAT IS HIDDEN

Reading and wrestling with the Daodejing offers a rare opportunity to step outside the assumptions of our received worldview. Most of the time, we move through life inside a framework we did not choose: one that emphasizes control, competition, efficiency, and progress. These values are so deeply woven into modern consciousness that they seem natural and inevitable. The Daodejing, however, presents a radically different way of seeing, a way that challenges the very premises of ambition, governance, morality, and even knowledge itself. It invites us to question whether striving leads to fulfillment, whether force leads to security, and whether rigid definitions lead to proper understanding.

The Daodejing works almost like a mirror that distorts the familiar, making what is usually hidden visible again. In doing so, it exposes the partiality of our usual ways of thinking and living. The text does not offer easy answers; it deliberately frustrates the desire for clear rules and systems. But this very frustration is part of its value. Wrestling, with its paradoxes and provocations, stretches our capacity to hold multiple perspectives, loosen our grip on certainty, and see that what we take as fixed is often contingent and constructed.

As a tool, the Daodejing doesn't simply critique; it creates openings. It reveals cracks in the armor of received ideas through which new light can enter. It shows other ways of being in the world, grounded not in domination or cleverness but in receptivity, patience, and trust in natural unfolding. In an era when many feel trapped in systems of their own making, struggling with the Daodejing can reawaken the imagination, allowing us to glimpse possibilities of life hidden beneath the weight of habit, fear, and cultural momentum.

PART ONE
DAO 道

CHAPTER I
SEEING DIFFERENTLY

We live in a world that we think we see clearly. But what if much of what we perceive isn't out there in the world but constructed inside our minds? What if perception isn't a window onto reality but a lens shaped by memory, language, emotion, and habit? This chapter is about learning to see differently — not just in the poetic sense, but in the intensely literal one. To walk the Way of Kinship, to live with a felt sense of interconnectedness, begins with this: recognizing that how we see shapes what we see, and what we see shapes how we act.

The Daodejing teaches us to attend to what is subtle, unforced, and often unseen. It asks us to release fixed ideas and social constructs so we can encounter the world more directly, with clarity and humility. These teachings are not abstract mysticism; they reflect something that modern cognitive science now affirms: perception is not a passive process. Our brains actively construct our experience, filtering and interpreting the world through layers of attention, interpretation, and embodied engagement. Understood in this way, perception is a practice that can be changed.

Adopting the perspective of the Way of Kinship is not simply swapping out one opinion for another. It requires a more profound transformation: a shift in how we attend to, interpret, and engage with the world. These three capacities — attention, interpretation, and engagement — form the core of perception. Change them, and your entire experience of reality begins to shift. Let's look at each of these in turn.

1. Attention

Attention is where it begins. What we notice (and what we overlook) shapes our world. If we're trained to focus only on utility, competition, or individual achievement, our lives will be filled with signs of scarcity and comparison. But when we begin to slow down and attend to relationships, patterns, and the subtleties of interdependence, we start to see a different world: one alive with mutual influence, silent cooperation, and hidden generosity. We notice the tree giving shade, the soil feeding the roots, or how another person's mood affects our own. This shift in attention allows us to feel kinship, not just understand it intellectually.

Cognitive science teaches us that perception is not a passive process of receiving information from the outside world; rather, it is an active and predictive process. The brain doesn't simply record data from the senses like a camera. Instead, it constructs reality by combining sensory input with prior expectations and beliefs. In short, we don't see the world as it is; we see it as our brains expect it to be, shaped by past experiences, cultural conditioning, and internal models. This means that changing how you perceive the world is not just about seeing new things; it's about updating the very models your brain uses to make sense of experience.

2. Interpretation

Next comes interpretation. What we see is never raw; it's always filtered through meaning. When we interpret things through a lens of control or fear, even neutral events can seem threatening or disappointing. But when we begin to interpret events in light of the Way of Kinship, we see setbacks as part of larger cycles and success as a shared emergence rather than a personal conquest. We stop dividing everything into "useful" or "useless," "winner" or "loser," and begin to see how things belong as part of a dynamic whole. Interpretation, in this sense, becomes an act of reintegration.

3. Engagement

Finally, engagement is where perception becomes embodied. How we relate to others, to nature, and to ourselves flows from what we attend to and how we interpret it. If we perceive the world as separate and adversarial, we engage with suspicion, effort, and control. However, when we perceive the world as interconnected and alive, we begin to engage with it with care, humility, and responsiveness. We stop trying to push outcomes and instead learn to move with the current, to participate rather than dominate. This is not a passive practice; it is an active one of attunement.

Our actions reinforce and shape our perceptions through what's known in neuroscience as sensorimotor feedback loops. When we act a certain way — whether it's rushing, forcing, or yielding — we create bodily and environmental feedback that our brains use to adjust future perceptions and behavior. This means that changing how we act in the world — even in small ways — gradually reshapes our perception and interpretation of it.

Imagine you're walking through a crowded city street, late for an appointment. You're rushing — weaving through people, scanning for gaps, shoulders tense, breath shallow. Your brain receives constant sensory input: the blur of people passing, snippets of impatient voices, the jostle of bodies brushing by. This hurried action amplifies a perception: "Everyone's in my way. This is stressful." The faster you go, the more your brain interprets the world as hostile and chaotic — reinforcing a sense of urgency and tension.

Now, picture choosing a different action. You deliberately slow your pace, drop your shoulders, take fuller breaths, and widen your gaze instead of narrowly focusing on the obstacles ahead. Your movement is more yielding than forcing. The sensory feedback shifts: you notice details — a street musician's melody, the rhythm of footsteps, the warmth of sunlight between buildings. This change in action doesn't just alter what you see; it changes how you interpret the experience. The same crowded street now feels less like an obstacle course and more like a living, dynamic environment.

This example is sensorimotor feedback at work. The way you move through the world literally feeds back into your nervous system, shaping how your brain perceives and interprets reality. Small changes in how we act — slowing down, softening our movements, yielding instead of forcing — can, over time, transform the very way we experience the world.

This chapter will continue with areas of attention that are key to the Daodejing. These include Absence and Presence, Transformation, and Patterns. As we become aware of these concepts, we start to notice them in our world. This is the first and most important step in walking the Way of Kinship. The following two sections will look at how we interpret our world through these new areas of attention. Then, part one concludes with engagement, how we begin to embody the Dao.

ATTENDING TO ABSENCE AND PRESENCE

Chapter 1 of the Daodejing introduces an important metaphysical relationship between absence (無 wú, pronounced "woo") and presence (有 yǒu, pronounced "yo"). These are not opposites in conflict but mutually dependent aspects of reality. Presence refers to what has form — things that can be named, seen, used, or known. On the other hand, absence has no form and cannot be named or grasped directly. But rather than nothingness in the sense of mere void or negation, absence is a generative emptiness, the fertile ground from which all things arise. This absence is not a lack but a source — a dynamic, unformed potential. Notice how they are presented in the opening chapter: "Absence names the origin of heaven and earth. Presence names the mother of the ten thousand things."

Here, absence is identified with the source — the beginning of all that exists before names, distinctions, or identities emerge. From this undifferentiated origin, form arises: the ten thousand things — a poetic way of referring to the world in all its diversity. Presence is born from absence, yet it is never entirely separate from it. All forms are transient; they emerge, take shape, and eventually dissolve. This transformation is not linear but cyclical: the movement from formlessness to form and back again.

> *The ten thousand things rise and fall while the*
> *self watches their return.*
> *They grow and flourish and then return to the*
> *source.*

Returning to the source is stillness, which is the
     way of nature.
The way of nature is unchanging.
(Chapter 16, Feng & English)

This cycle — emergence and return — lies at the heart of the Daodejing's vision of how the world works. Things come into being through a subtle unfolding from the unmanifest, and they return to it when their time passes. This is not a tragedy or loss but a natural rhythm. To understand absence and presence is to understand the dance of existence — that everything we see, use, and name is temporary. Yet, it is grounded in something enduring and ever-present precisely because it cannot be grasped.

Thirty spokes together form a hub
Its emptiness (無 wú) is necessary
To have (有 yǒu) a useful cart.
Mold clay into a vessel
Its emptiness (無 wú) is necessary
To have (有 yǒu) a useful vessel.
Construct doors and windows into a room
Their emptiness (無 wú) is necessary
To have (有 yǒu) a useful room.
Therefore,
To have (有 yǒu) makes benefit
Emptiness (無 wú) makes useful.
(Chapter 11)

This passage from chapter 11 of the Daodejing tells us

that emptiness has value — the space within allows it to function. Similarly, the unseen and unformed play a crucial role in shaping the visible and functional world.

The implication is clear: to live wisely is to remain aware of both presence and absence, form and the formless source from which form arises. We must not become so enchanted by the visible world that we forget what sustains it. The Daodejing invites us to cultivate sensitivity to the unspoken, the unseen, and the unresolved — to appreciate not only what things are but also where they come from and where they return. In this way, absence is not the opposite of life but its ground, the silent partner in all becoming.

These insights into absence and presence did not arise from metaphysical guesswork or mystical abstraction. They emerged from careful, attentive observation of the world — of how things grow, decay, appear, and vanish. The early Daoist sages were embedded within nature, studying its patterns through direct experience. This kind of observation invites a different mode of understanding — not one that imposes rigid categories onto the world, but one that listens and watches for the subtle rhythms at work. To recognize that presence arises from absence is to begin seeing the world as a set of unfolding relationships rather than isolated things.

Thus, the concepts of absence and presence are not speculative metaphysics; they are distilled from a long tradition of attunement to nature — how clouds form, rivers flow, and creatures adapt. What makes these ideas enduring is precisely their grounding in lived reality. They reflect a worldview that trusts the patterns of the world more than human constructions and invites us to live in greater alignment with the source of things rather than their surface appearances. In this way, the Daodejing speaks not only as a philosophy but as a kind of ecological wisdom — a reminder that if we look deeply and quietly at the world, it will show us how it works.

What makes the Daodejing especially radical is that it recognizes the interplay between absence and presence, often prioritizing absence. The priority of absence runs counter to the common human tendency to focus on what is visible, tangible, and nameable — the things that stand out in the foreground of experience. Daoist thought invites us to reverse this orientation. It suggests that what is essential is what we do not see, what supports and surrounds the obvious but goes unremarked. The empty space in a bowl is what makes it useful. The stillness between movements gives rhythm its meaning. The silence between words allows language to be heard.

This sensitivity to the background, to what is not immediately apparent, is a hallmark of Daoist perception. The authors who composed the Daodejing were attentive to events and the conditions that enabled those events to occur. Just as the night sky allows stars to shine, absence provides the context in which presence becomes meaningful. To live in tune with the Dao means cultivating a broader awareness: seeing not only what is in front of us, but also what surrounds it, precedes it, and enables it. It requires a kind of peripheral vision — the ability to notice the space behind the form, the silence beneath sound, the stillness inside the action. Chapter 1 of the Daodejing calls us to reflect deeply on both absence and presence as a means to grasp the context of reality:

> *Focus on enduring absence by observing its*
>   *mystery,*
> *Focus on enduring presence by observing its*
>   *manifestations,*
> *[Until] both are unified (although they differ in*
>   *name).*
> *Call this unity darkness,*
> *Darkness within darkness,*
> *The entrance to all mysteries.*
> *(Chapter 1)*

The Daodejing does not deny the value of what appears; rather, it reminds us that appearance is dependent. Forms rise and fall. Names come and go. What endures is the open source from which all things emerge and to which all things return. In this way, absence is not only prior in time but in ontological importance: it is the condition of possibility for everything we perceive and name. By shifting our attention toward the background — to the quiet, the open, the unformed — we begin to participate in a deeper rhythm that aligns us with the unfolding of the world rather than standing apart from it.

OBSERVING TRANSFORMATION

The Daodejing contains numerous observations about the way things in the world tend to transform into their opposites. Things do not remain in a fixed state. High becomes low, strong becomes weak, and success turns into failure. These reversals are not exceptional events but regular features of how life unfolds.

One of the most direct expressions of this idea appears in Chapter 58, where the text says,

> *Bad fortune rests upon good fortune.*
> *Good luck hides within bad luck.*
> *(Addiss & Lombardo)*

This observation suggests that situations contain within them the seeds of their reversal. What seems secure today may give way tomorrow. What appears unfortunate may turn out to be a turning point. The Daodejing does not present this as irony or tragedy but simply as the way of things. The conditions that lead to flourishing can give rise to collapse if they are pushed too far. The more complete something becomes, the more it begins to decline.

Another example is found in Chapter 9:

> *Better stop short than fill to the brim.*
> *Over sharpen the blade, and the edge will soon*
> *   blunt."*
> *(Feng & English)*

Here, the observation is about excess leading to loss. There is an implied point of balance, after which continuing to accumulate, push, or refine becomes counterproductive. Overreaching leads to reversal not because of punishment or fate but because that is how things behave when they are stretched beyond their limits.

The text has a recurring theme of hidden instability within stability. Situations that seem successful or dominant are often close to their decline. In Chapter 36, the text notes,

> *That which fails*
> *Must first be strong.*
> *That which is cast down*
> *Must first be raised.*
> *(Feng & English)*

The pattern observed here is not linear progress but a cyclical or pendulum-like motion, where extreme states tend to revert to their opposite state. The force that pushes something in one direction eventually gives way to a counterforce, not from outside but from within the situation itself.

These passages encourage caution and attentiveness. The Daodejing presents a world in which no condition is final, and every position contains the beginning of its reversal. Understanding this helps one move with the world rather than be caught off guard by its turns. The sage is described as someone who recognizes this flux and, therefore, does not cling to outcomes or rush to extremes. In observing how things transform into their opposites, the text invites a way of living that is more responsive, restrained, and in rhythm with the natural movement of things.

NOTICING PATTERNS

The careful observation and attention to nature revealed the patterns of absence, presence, and transformation. Sometimes, the most ordinary concepts carry the most profound implications. Patterns are one of those concepts. They're so deeply woven into our experience that we often overlook them — yet they structure everything from our habits to the fabric of the cosmos. A pattern is a repeated or recurring arrangement of elements — sounds, shapes, behaviors, or events — that follow some recognizable order. Patterns allow us to discover the coherence in what otherwise looks like chaos. They enable us to anticipate, adapt, and act. In many respects, the philosophy of the Daodejing is a profound meditation on the dynamics of patterns as living rhythms that emerge, transform, and harmonize the world around us. The Dao, the way, can be understood as the way of things, the patterns of the universe.

Patterns Make Learning Possible

. . .

What does it mean to learn something? This is a question that has long preoccupied me. Learning is the process of recognizing patterns and internalizing them to make reliable predictions. To learn is to become attuned to regularities in experience. At first, this might sound overly abstract, but consider a simple case: imagine you've never encountered fire before. Curious, you reach your hand toward a flame, and pain jolts you backward. You try again, and once more, the flame burns. You've discovered a predictable pattern: fire burns. This realization now shapes your future behavior. You've learned.

The capacity to perceive and retain patterns is foundational to how we operate in the world. Without patterns, learning wouldn't just be difficult; it would be impossible. There would be no basis for memory, no consistency to inform behavior, no cause-and-effect relationships to build on. Our ability to speak a language, compose music, cook a meal, solve problems, or form relationships rests on patterned interactions. Learning is not merely memorizing isolated facts but rather discovering meaningful regularities that help us navigate reality creatively and effectively.

Patterns make learning possible because they are persistent. If fire sometimes burned and sometimes did not, there would be no way to form a reliable expectation and thus no basis for meaningful understanding. The fact that patterns hold is what allows us to live in an intelligible world.

This insight is at the heart of science. Science is not a catalog of facts but a disciplined search for underlying patterns across matter, motion, life, and behavior. From the spin of subatomic particles to the behavior of social groups, science is a methodology for finding the repeatable, the generalizable, and the predictive. It assumes that the world is not arbitrary — that something about it is stable enough to be known. In this sense, the world is not only knowable but patterned in ways that invite understanding.

Patterns Make Existence Possible

But patterns are not just helpful for human understanding — they are essential to the existence of anything at all. At the most fundamental level, what we call "physical laws" are really discovered patterns: predictable, stable interactions that give rise to atoms, molecules, and the large-scale structures of stars, planets, and living organisms. If these fundamental patterns didn't repeat exactly — if the electromagnetic force or the behavior of gravity were inconsistent — nothing would cohere. No atom would form, no organism could persist, no event would be repeatable. The existence of regularity is not an incidental feature of the universe — it is the precondition for any coherent structure to exist.

The Daodejing hints at this kind of deep ontological patterning: the idea that the world arises through the dynamic interplay of forces (yin and yang, absence and presence) that cycle and return. Patterns are not just a cognitive tool but the rhythm of becoming itself.

. . .

Patterns Make an Interconnected World

Patterns don't exist in isolation. Every pattern is affected by — and affects — other patterns. This interactivity creates a web of relationships where no event or element exists in isolation. In this sense, the world is not just patterned but interconnected. A change in one place ripples outward, shaping modifications elsewhere. This is a truth we are slowly relearning in the context of ecology, where the balance of an ecosystem depends on countless interconnected relationships, each influencing the other in a dynamic whole. To live well, then, is to live in awareness of these interconnections — to act in harmony with the patterns that sustain life rather than disrupt them.

CHAPTER 2

INTERPRETATION

After adjusting our attention by attending to absence and presence, observing transformation, and noticing patterns, we now shift to interpretation. What implications can we draw from this fresh view of the world? The following two sections will address co-dependent origination and the concept of co-action. Here, I start with a framework for interpreting the world called yinyang.

YINYANG

The symbol most associated with Daoism is called the taijitu (太極圖 tài-jí-tú, pronounced tie-jee-too) or the yinyang (陰陽 yīn-yáng, pronounced yin-yong), and it depicts a unique form of balance. Although this is only mentioned once in chapter 42 of the Daodejing, its meaning runs throughout.

The yinyang symbol shows a circle divided into two flowing, interpenetrating shapes: one black (yin) and one white (yang), each containing a small dot of the other's color. The flowing division between the black and white sides is curved, not straight, emphasizing that yin and yang are not rigidly separate but dynamically related. They are constantly moving, transforming into one another. The presence of the black dot in the white area and the white dot in the black area shows that the seed of the opposite is already present within each phase. At the peak of yang's fullness, yin begins to emerge; at the depth of yin, yang is already stirring.

The entire symbol forms a circle, an emerging thirdness from the two. A dynamic, emergent unity arises from yin and yang interaction. This thirdness is not a static midpoint or compromise but a creative, living outcome of the relational process between the two. The dynamic interplay of yin and yang produces something new: an evolving wholeness that cannot be reduced to either yin or yang alone. An ongoing, emergent balance that is continually responsive, adaptive, and alive. Thus, thirdness reflects the insight that the world is not composed of rigid binaries but of fluid relationships that continuously generate new configurations of reality. It emphasizes creativity, transformation, and interdependence over opposition or fixed categories. In this sense, thirdness helps deepen the understanding of yinyang as a generative and relational model of reality, not merely a theory of opposites. (For more on the idea of thirdness, see Robin R. Wang's *Yin Yang: The Way of Heaven and Earth in Chinese Thought and Culture*)

Understanding this symbol means learning to live with fluidity, with awareness of timing, balance, and change, rather than rigidly clinging to one side or resisting the inevitable movements of life. Rather than thinking of yin and yang as two opposing forces locked in conflict, they are complementary aspects of a continuous process: dark and light, stillness and movement, receptivity and activity. Each gives rise to the other, depends on the other, and transforms into the other.

Yin and yang are not fixed substances or moral categories. Instead, they describe how change happens: balance, interaction, and alternation. When one aspect reaches its extreme, it naturally gives way to the other. For example, the deepest night (yin) turns into dawn (yang), and the hottest midday (yang) declines into evening (yin). In human life, strength (yang) must be tempered by softness (yin), action by rest, and assertion by yielding. Harmony is not achieved by choosing one side over the other but by understanding their rhythm and adjusting oneself accordingly.

To live wisely is to sense these movements and act in tune with the shifting balances of life rather than resisting them or imposing rigid structures. It is to trust that life, like the interaction of yin and yang, has its own intelligence, requiring not domination but sensitive responsiveness.

Yin is associated with darkness, coolness, softness, stillness, yielding, the feminine, the earth, the receptive, and the inward. It is linked to the moon, the night, and the unseen forces that nurture and sustain.

Yang is associated with brightness, heat, hardness,

activity, firmness, the masculine, the heavens, the active, and the outward. It is linked to the sun, the day, and the visible forces that create movement and structure.

From this broad foundation, a deeper layer of understanding emerges: yin represents not just passivity but potential — the rich, undefined, emerging source from which new forms arise. It is the mystery of things not yet shaped, the novel, the unexplored, the chaotic vitality of beginnings. Yang, by contrast, represents definition and control: the establishment of form, order, structure, and predictability. It is the known world, the mapped terrain, and the systems we impose to stabilize the swirling unknown.

Thus, yin can be seen as the principle of chaos, not in a purely negative sense, but as the fertile ground of newness, creativity, and possibility. Yang is the principle of control, not in a purely oppressive sense, but as the force that organizes, clarifies, and makes the world navigable. Both are necessary. Too much yin leads to dissolution and confusion; too much yang leads to rigidity and brittleness. True vitality comes from the ongoing, skillful balance between the wild, creative unknown and the stabilizing, shaping known.

Yinyang, at its heart, expresses the profound interdependence and mutual influence of all things. Yin and yang are not separate entities battling for dominance; they are interdependent aspects of a single unfolding reality. Each exists only in relation to the other. There is no concept of darkness without light, no stillness without motion, no yielding without firmness. Interdependence and mutual influence reflect the deeper understanding that everything is ultimately one interconnected process manifesting in various configurations and patterns. Yin and yang continually generate and transform each other, and every shift in their balance ripples outward. Nothing changes in isolation; just as a movement in one part of a spider's web affects the entire structure, every transformation within yin or yang subtly reshapes the whole system. This vision dissolves the illusion of separateness, revealing that life is not made up of isolated things but of continuous, dynamic relationships — an ever-changing dance of mutual arising, influence, and transformation.

CO-DEPENDENT ORIGINATION

The Way of Kinship shapes the interpretive lens through which we see the world. Interconnectedness is a core component of that lens, but deeper still is the concept of co-dependent origination.

The concept of co-dependent origination represents a profound shift in our understanding of existence. Rather than seeing the world as composed of separate, self-contained things interacting with one another, co-dependent origination suggests that things do not exist independently at all. Instead, everything comes into being through relationships. Nothing has an isolated, permanent essence; it emerges through context, interaction, and change. In the Daodejing, nothing stands alone; everything arises as part of a web of patterned interdependence.

The Daodejing does not explicitly use the term "co-dependent origination." Still, its vision of reality is entirely aligned with it. Chapter after chapter describes how opposites arise together — long and short, high and low, before and after. But these are not mere contrasts; they are mutually defining. There is no "long" without "short" to compare it to. There is no "high" without a "low." These qualities do not preexist their relationship — they emerge through it. Ultimately, all of the attributes we use to describe something (size, weight, shape, color, speed) only exist in relationship to something else.

Modern physics — particularly the relational interpretation of quantum mechanics — echoes this insight in surprising ways. In relational quantum theory, the properties of any object do not exist in a fixed, observer-independent way. Instead, properties such as position, momentum, or even identity only have meaning in relation to something else, typically an observer or another system. There is no absolute "state of the world"; there are only interactions, and it is through those interactions that the world takes shape. In his book *The Order of Time*, Carlo Rovelli states, "The world is not a collection of things. It is a collection of events" (p. 98). This deeply resonates with the Daoist view that reality is not composed of discrete objects but of unfolding relationships.

Co-dependent origination is not just a metaphysical idea — it has ethical and existential consequences. If nothing exists on its own, then neither do we. Our identity, well-being, and meaning arise from our connection to others, to the land, and to the invisible networks of support that sustain us. This view challenges the modern fixation on autonomy and control. It invites humility — not the kind that devalues the self, but the kind that situates the self within a larger living system. In this way, co-dependent origination is not merely a truth about how things are; it is a call to live with responsiveness, reciprocity, and reverence.

The Way of Kinship, as expressed in this book, is built on this understanding. It is the recognition that everything we do touches everything else and that our lives are possible only because of the vast, unseen cooperation of the world. To see this clearly is not only to think differently — it is to feel differently, to move differently, and to walk with the kind of presence that knows we are never separate.

If nothing exists independently, then it follows that nothing is fixed or final either. From this insight arises a more profound understanding: everything is a process. Things are not solid, self-contained entities moving through time; instead, they are events, patterns of change unfolding through relationships. This is the essence of process philosophy, a view of reality that emphasizes becoming over being, movement over stasis, and relation over essence.

In this view, what we call a "thing" — a person, a tree, even a mountain — is better understood as a continuity of transformations rather than a permanent object with a stable identity. A person is not a fixed self, but an ongoing pattern of physical, emotional, and cognitive activity shaped by history, environment, and interaction. A tree is not just a form standing still in space but a process of photosynthesis, growth, decay, and renewal — embedded in the flow of seasons, soil chemistry, and ecological networks. Each so-called object is, in fact, a node in a web of unfolding activity.

This perspective reshapes how we understand not only nature but ethics, identity, and knowledge. If everything is a process, then to know something is not to define it once and for all but to participate in its unfolding. To live well is not to control or perfect the self but to continually adapt, respond, and flow with the shifting conditions of life. The Daodejing gestures toward this sensibility throughout, not with formal theory but via its recurring images of water, softness, return, and transformation. These images point toward a world where form is never static, and the wise live by aligning themselves with the ever-changing stream of reality.

Process philosophy, in both its ancient and modern forms, calls us to let go of the illusion of solidity — in ourselves, in others, and in the world. Instead, it invites us to cultivate presence within movement and clarity within change. To see everything as a process is to recognize that life is not made of things but of relations in motion — and that wisdom lies in learning how to move with them.

ALL ACTION IS CO-ACTION

If all things arise through co-dependent origination, and all things are fundamentally processes rather than fixed substances, then action cannot be thought of as originating solely from isolated individuals or discrete causes. Instead, every action is, in truth, a co-action — an event that emerges from the interplay of multiple conditions. Whether a leaf falls, a decision is made, or a word is spoken, that event is never purely the result of a single agent. It is the outcome of interactions between countless forces: context, history, environment, culture, biology, memory, and more. Nothing acts alone, and nothing arises in isolation.

From this perspective, all action is inter-action. Even what we usually label as a "personal choice" is shaped by an immense web of influences that extend far beyond conscious intention. My decision to speak, move, or think in a certain way is not just mine — it is the result of a vast set of prior conditions and relational forces. These might include language I did not invent, emotions shaped by others, and inherited patterns I did not choose. My action is more like a wave forming in the current of a river than a pebble thrown into still water. The wave cannot exist apart from the flow.

This leads naturally to a deeper reflection on determinism. If every event is the result of interacting processes — and if those processes are themselves shaped by other processes — then the idea of a genuinely independent cause begins to dissolve. Determinism, in this context, does not mean mechanical fatalism or predestination. It means that what happens is always the result of what came before and what is happening now. The universe unfolds as a continuous stream of interrelated activity. Nothing stands outside this unfolding, and nothing escapes its momentum.

Determinism is often misunderstood as a kind of existential trap — the idea that if everything is caused, then nothing can truly change. But this view misses a crucial truth: change is only possible because the universe is patterned. Without reliable patterns — in matter, energy, behavior, or thought — there would be no continuity, no stability, no existence at all. If atoms didn't hold together the same way each time, if gravity didn't pull predictably, or if memory didn't retain structure, there would be no coherent world, no life, and no mind to ask questions about freedom or fate.

It is precisely because the universe operates through consistent patterns that change becomes meaningful and possible. Patterns don't lock us into repetition; they provide the framework within which transformation occurs. A melody is not a cage because it follows a structure — it is expressive because of it. In the same way, when we observe a pattern, whether in nature, behavior, or society, we gain the ability to work with it. To know a pattern is to find leverage. In a deterministic world, understanding how something arises allows us to see how it might change. Our recognition of the pattern becomes part of the pattern, influencing what comes next.

This leads to a more subtle view of action. What we do is not the result of an unconditioned will standing outside the cosmos. Instead, our actions emerge from who we are, and who we are is a confluence of conditions: biology, history, relationships, environment, and learning. We are not autonomous agents floating above causality — we are living systems embedded within it, capable of reflection and adjustment. Our choices arise not from randomness but from the deep patterns that have shaped our understanding, intentions, and desires. And that is precisely what we want:

for our actions to express who we are rather than being arbitrary or disconnected from context.

What distinguishes human agency is not its freedom from causation but its capacity to learn, anticipate, and reshape patterns. We are learning systems — adaptive, responsive, and capable of transforming our internal structures in response to new information. This is not a loophole in determinism; it is its profoundest expression. In every moment, we are the location where countless streams of influence meet, and from that convergence, something new unfolds. Our ability to observe, understand, and respond is not a violation of the pattern — it is the evolution of the pattern through us.

Imagine you're offered a new job in a different city. At first glance, it feels like a personal choice: "Do I take it or stay?" But if you slow down and look closely, you can see how this moment of decision is actually the convergence of countless conditions.

Your willingness to even consider the move has roots in childhood experiences — maybe you grew up watching your parents adapt to new places, or perhaps you once promised yourself you'd leave your hometown. Your confidence to apply came from teachers and mentors who encouraged you years ago, the books you've read, the skills you've practiced, and the encouragement of a close friend who believed you were ready for more. Even the job itself exists because of economic shifts, company needs, and a cultural moment that values your expertise. The city you might move to has been shaped by history, infrastructure, and communities you've never met but who will soon influence you.

When you say "yes" or "no," that action doesn't arise from a single, isolated will. It's like a wave forming in a river — the natural expression of everything upstream: your biology, education, relationships, cultural norms, emotional state, and even your body's physical responses to stress and opportunity. And when you make your choice, that action doesn't just end with you. It ripples outward — reshaping your relationships, impacting the company, influencing how others see their own possibilities.

Seen this way, your decision isn't diminished. It's more profound. You're not floating outside of causation, but standing at the meeting point of countless streams, adding your weight, your learning, and your intention to the current — and watching a new pattern emerge.

In this view, to act wisely is not to transcend causality but to become more intimate with it — to know what leads to what, to see the deeper forces at play, and to participate skillfully in the unfolding. We are not outside the world directing it. We are the point at which the world becomes conscious of itself, and in that consciousness, a new kind of co-action becomes possible.

CHAPTER 3
ENGAGEMENT

The character 道 (dào) is composed of two parts: the radical 辶 (chuò), which means "to walk" or "movement," and the phonetic component 首 (shǒu), meaning "head" or "leader." Together, they convey the idea of a path one follows, or more broadly, a way or course along which something moves or develops. In its most basic sense, 道 refers to a road, path, or route — something physical or metaphorical that can be walked, followed, or traveled. By extension, it came to signify a way of doing things, a method, or even a principle that guides action. The structure of the character captures both directionality (the journey or movement) and guidance (what leads or shows the way), making it a rich term even in non-philosophical contexts. People would speak of the dao of farming, cooking, or traveling, meaning the typical or proper way to go about those tasks. It was a common, practical term used to describe the flow or direction of things in daily life — a familiar and flexible word before it took on more abstract and philosophical meanings in later texts.

DAO EXPLORED

The Dao of the Daodejing can be thought of as the underlying way, process, or pattern that gives rise to everything in the universe. It is not a deity or a force to command; it is the natural unfolding of reality itself — the spontaneous, self-organizing principle through which all things come into being, change, and pass away. In the Daodejing, Dao is both the source and the path: it is the silent origin of existence and the way things move and flourish when left unforced. Notably, the Dao is not something outside or separate from the world.

Living according to the Dao means recognizing the rhythms of life — understanding when to act and when to yield, when to speak and when to remain silent, when to intervene, and when to let things take their natural course. It is a way of being that values simplicity, humility, and adaptability over force, ambition, and control. In the Daodejing, the sage does not seek to conquer the world but to move harmoniously within it, trusting that the Dao is always at work, even (and especially) when human plans fail.

In this sense, the Dao of the Daodejing offers a deep alternative to the human impulse to dominate, categorize, and control. It invites us to enter life's flowing patterns with

attentiveness and reverence, allowing the hidden order of
things to reveal itself naturally over time.

The Daodejing employs a series of vivid metaphors to
guide readers toward understanding the Dao. Here are a few
of the most important:

- Water is perhaps the most central metaphor for
  the Dao. Water yields to every obstacle — it
  flows around rocks, fills valleys, seeks the lowest
  places — yet it wears down the hardest stone
  over time. It is gentle and humble yet supremely
  powerful. Like water, the Dao is soft, flexible,
  and nurturing, yet it accomplishes
  transformation without force. The Daodejing
  urges us to be like water, valuing softness,
  adaptability, and persistence over aggression.

  The highest adeptness is like water.
  Water's adeptness benefits the ten thousand
       things without contending.
  [Water] resides where humans abhor.
  In doing so, [water] resembles Dao.
  (Chapter 8)

- Uncarved wood symbolizes original simplicity
  and wholeness — things in their natural,
  untouched state. As uncarved wood holds
  endless potential before being shaped by human
  hands, the Dao is the undivided source of all
  things before they are fragmented by human

naming and categorizing. Carving wood is an image that depicts forcing something into an artificial shape, often referring to people being forced into artificial social structures. Cultivating uncarved wood means returning to simplicity, humility, and openness, resisting the urge to impose rigid structures or excessive refinement.

Banish learning, discard knowledge: People will
     gain a hundredfold.
Banish benevolence, discard righteousness:
     People will return to duty and compassion.
Banish skill, discard profit: There will be no more
     thieves.
These three statements are not enough.
One more step is necessary:
Look at plain silk; hold uncarved wood.
The self dwindles; desires fade.
(Chapter 19, Addiss & Lombardo)

- The valley is low, receptive, and nourishing. It accepts everything without resistance and sustains life through its emptiness. In the Daodejing, being like a valley means embracing emptiness, humility, and openness. The valley metaphor emphasizes that genuine strength lies in receptivity and the ability to contain and support rather than dominate.

The valley spirit does not die.

It is called the dark female/mother.
The entrance of the dark female/mother,
is called the source of Heaven and Earth.
[The source is] continuous, seeming to exist.
Using [the generative potential] does not require
*   force/effort.*
(Chapter 8)

- The newborn child is another metaphor for alignment with the Dao. Infants are soft, supple, and free from rigid concepts. They embody vitality and potential because ambition, control, or pride have not yet shaped them. The Daodejing suggests that maintaining childlike flexibility and trust in life is essential for living in accordance with the Dao.

    Gather your qi to attain suppleness,
    can you be like a child?
    (Chapter 10)

Each of these metaphors reveals a facet of the Dao's nature: yielding without weakness, nurturing without domination, being simple and flexible rather than rigid and proud. Together, they form a language of imagery that invites the reader not just to understand the Dao intellectually but to sense it intuitively and to live in alignment with it.

. . .

In the teachings of Confucius (孔子, Kǒngzǐ), the Dao is more human-centered. It refers to the Way of proper moral conduct, social harmony, and cultivated virtue. The Dao for Confucius is embodied in the rituals, ethical relationships, and inherited traditions that structure society. It is not a wild, cosmic flow to be yielded to but a pattern of righteous behavior to be learned, practiced, and refined. The Confucian sage actively engages with the world, striving to improve society by embodying and teaching virtues such as loyalty, respect, and propriety.

Thus, where the Daodejing sees the Dao as the spontaneous Way of the cosmos, best approached by letting go of human striving, Confucianism sees the Dao as the cultivated Way of human society, requiring active moral and social effort. The Daodejing views human interference, ambition, and artificial structure as sources of disorder, while Confucians see human cultivation, education, and ritual as the means to create harmony.

In the Analects, Confucius links the Dao directly to moral cultivation and social order:

> Lead the people with administrative injunctions
>   and keep them orderly with penal law, and
>   they will avoid punishments but will be
>   without a sense of shame. Lead them with
>   virtue and keep them orderly through
>   observing ritual, and they will develop a
>   sense of shame, and moreover, will order
>   themselves.
> (Analects 2:3, Lau)

Here, the Way (Dao) is human-centered — realized through deliberate moral education and the performance of rituals (禮, lǐ). The Confucian sage works to shape people and society through cultivated behavior, using inherited traditions as tools for reform. The Dao is something to practice and embody within the structures of human relationships.

In contrast, the Daodejing warns against imposing rigid order:

> *The more laws and restrictions there are,*
> *the poorer the people become.*
> *The sharper men's weapons,*
> *the more troubled the land.*
> *The more ingenious and clever people are,*
> *the more strange things happen.*
> *The more rules and regulations,*
> *the more thieves and robbers.*
> *(Daodejing 57, Feng & English)*

Here, the Dao is portrayed as the spontaneous, self-regulating Way of the cosmos. Social overengineering — laws, rules, cleverness — disrupts natural harmony. Instead of seeking to reform people through imposed morality, the sage in the Daodejing steps back, allowing order to emerge organically by aligning with the underlying patterns of Dao.

Together, these passages show the philosophical divergence: Confucius sees order arising from human cultivation and structure, while Laozi sees order emerging from non-coercive alignment with the natural Way.

The Daodejing is often in dialogue with the conventional wisdom of the day, especially with the philosophy of the Confucians. This is powerfully evident in the opening chapter. Now that we have a fuller understanding of the concept of Dao, I will look in detail at chapter one, which serves as an overture to the whole of the Daodejing. In what follows, I will show the original Chinese and my translation. Next, I will go into a detailed line-by-line explanation. In only chapter one and thirty-eight of the Daodejing do I go into this level of detail. These two chapters represent the two main sections of the Daodejing: Dao, chapters 1-37, and De, chapters 38-81.

CHAPTER 4
DAODEJING ONE

ORIGINAL TEXT

1道可道非常道
dào kě dào fēi cháng dào

2名可名非常名
míng kě míng fēi cháng míng

3無名天地之始
wú míng tiān dì zhī shǐ

4有名萬物之母
yǒu míng wàn wù zhī mǔ

故
gù

5 常無欲以觀其妙
cháng wúyù yǐ guān qí miào

6 常有欲以觀其徼
cháng yǒu yù yǐ guān qí jiào

7 此兩者同出而異名
cǐ liǎng zhě tóng chū ér yì míng

8 同謂之玄
tóng wèi zhī xuán

9 玄之又玄
xuán zhī yòu xuán

10 眾妙之門
zhòng miào zhī mén

TRANSLATION

*1. A Dao that can be followed is not the enduring
    Dao.*

2. Names can name no enduring name.

3. Absence names the origin of heaven and earth.

*4. Presence names the mother of the ten
    thousand things.*

Therefore:

*5. Focus on enduring absence by observing its
    mystery,*

*6. Focus on enduring presence by observing its
    manifestations,*

*7. [Until] both are unified (although they differ
    in name).*

8. Call this unity darkness,

9. Darkness within darkness,

10. The entrance to all mysteries.

DETAILED COMMENTS

Line (1)

The opening line is simple in its wording but complex in its interpretation. A literal translation is:

Dao can Dao, not enduring Dao.

I usually leave Dao untranslated because it carries a meaning beyond the basic English translation of "way." For now, I will use "way" to make it easier to see what is happening with this line:

Way can Way, not enduring Way.

In Chinese, a character can be a noun or a verb, depending on the context. Here, it would need to be something like:

A way that can be wayed, is not the enduring way.

"Wayed" is not a word in English. The idea of "waying" would be "following" or "followed," which is how my translation reads:

A Dao that can be followed is not the enduring Dao.

If you have read any other translations of the Daodejing, you will notice that many, if not the majority of translations, say something like: "The Dao that can be spoken of is not the constant Dao." This is not incorrect, and we will see how one arrives at that translation, but I find "spoken" misleading as to what the line is trying to convey. Using "spoken of" implies that the Dao cannot be expressed in words, which seems to be supported by the second line: Names can name no enduring name. While I agree that the Dao cannot be fully expressed in words, there is a more significant meaning that these two lines are trying to convey. Also, it would be odd to open a book about the Dao by stating that you can't really say anything about the Dao.

Notice that line (1) tells us that two concepts of Dao are being contrasted. First is the Dao that can be followed or spoken of, and second is the enduring Dao. Whatever the first Dao is, it is different from the second Dao. So, where do these different Daos come from?

The historical context of the Daodejing is the Warring States period — a time of great social chaos. This period in Chinese history gave rise to multiple philosophies known as the Hundred Schools of Thought. Each of these schools addressed, in one way or another, the question: What brought us to this time of social chaos, and what is the way out? The schools each offered a Way, a Dao, as the solution. The first and most prominent school was the philosophy of Confucius. For Confucius, the way out involved returning to and upholding the correct and longstanding traditions that held Chinese culture together, exemplified at the peak of the

Zhou dynasty. You can think of Confucius' Dao as instructions to be followed that would result in social harmony if everyone played their part.

In his teachings (as recorded in the Analects), Confucius often appeals to the ancient sages — especially figures like King Wen, King Wu, and the Duke of Zhou — as models of proper virtue, governance, and ritual. Here, Confucius states that the insights he teaches are not his own, but rather what he has learned from the ancients:

> *Transmitting insight, but never creating insight,*
> *standing by my words and devoted to the*
> *ancients.*
> (Analects 7.1, Hinton)

For Confucius, Dao was a specific cultural inheritance — the correct rites, music, governance, and ethical norms — practiced by ancient virtuous rulers. His project was thus restorative: to preserve, study, and reapply these early Zhou traditions, which he saw as the correct expressions of moral truth in human society.

Line (1) challenges the "correct tradition" concept of Dao. As a tradition, Dao can be spoken (as a means to transmit the instruction), and one can follow the tradition. Only in this sense should we translate as "spoken" rather than "follow." The issue, though, is not that the Dao is inexpressible; the issue is with the concept of the Dao as a correct tradition.

· · ·

I take some time to explain this opening line in detail because how we translate this line changes the focus of the entire book. The translations that, in various ways, state that the Dao cannot be "spoken of" set the stage for an esoteric wisdom of self-reflection, and all the many passages that deal with political issues are assumed to be metaphors for how we govern ourselves. It removes the Daodejing from its historical context. It turns it into a timeless truth, which can be interpreted to mean just about anything. Only when we keep the Daodejing firmly in its historical context do we have any hope of getting at what the original authors were trying to convey. When we understand this opening line as confronting a contrary concept of Dao, explicitly addressing social arrangements and the consequences of prolonged war, the other political references in the Daodejing fall into place. There is still plenty of room for self-reflection, but now we have concrete examples of confronting social norms and ways of looking at the world that we can use to address the social concerns we face today. Our world is also rich in social traditions, encompassing religion, culture, economics, and national identity. There is much to learn from this ancient wisdom of resistance.

Before turning to how the concept of Dao is understood in the Daodejing, I want to clarify why I use the phrase "correct tradition" when describing the Confucian view. Confucius did not advocate for tradition in a general sense — he wasn't suggesting that any custom or inherited practice would do. Instead, he pointed to a specific tradition rooted in the early Zhou dynasty — the ancient sages' rites, norms, and moral practices — as the authentic expression of the Dao, the Way.

However, this raises an important question: how can we determine that this tradition is the correct one among all the other options? The difficulty is that the justification for its correctness tends to rest within the tradition itself. Confucian thought appeals to the authority of the sages and the continuity of ritual as proof of legitimacy. Yet this creates a kind of circular reasoning: the tradition is correct because the tradition says so. And if one steps outside of that circle to justify it — appealing to reason, utility, or nature, for example — then it would be those external criteria, not the tradition itself, that ground its authority. In that case, the tradition becomes secondary, or even dispensable, relative to whatever standard is used to validate it.

This is the conceptual trap: if you rely solely on tradition to prove its truth, you appeal to a closed system. But if you appeal to something outside of it, you undermine the tradition's claim to being the exclusive or definitive expression of the Dao. The Daodejing authors challenge this tension between tradition as self-justifying and the need for an independent standard head-on.

The Daodejing questions whether any fixed human tradition could truly capture lived reality. It asks: How can we know that the practices of the past genuinely reflect what we should do? Even if the ancient sages understood something profound, the conditions of their era differed significantly from those of the present. Each situation emerges uniquely from the flow of life, and any attempt to codify the "right" way risks severing us from direct engagement with the world as it is.

The Daodejing is skeptical of the appeal to authority central to Confucian thought. Rather than encouraging genuine understanding, reliance on the pronouncements of ancient figures substitutes imitation for authentic insight. The enduring Dao cannot be handed down by decree; it must be encountered freshly through attunement to the shifting patterns of nature and human experience.

Finally, because a tradition cannot be shown to be objectively true without appealing to something beyond the tradition, one has the problem of enforcement. Confucians sought to maintain social harmony by enforcing correct behavior through education, ritual, and sometimes law. However, this effort to control social values was self-defeating. As the Daodejing teaches, the more rules and prohibitions a society imposes, the more disorder it invites. Attempts to correct human behavior by imposing external standards alienate people from their innate capacity for balance and harmony. In contrast to the Confucian project of molding society according to a sacred tradition, the Daodejing advocates for trust in the spontaneous unfolding of life.

When Dao is understood as a tradition, it focuses on the realm of human interaction and how we structure society. What is unique to the Daodejing is that it elevates the concept of Dao to a cosmic level. Dao is not simply the way for humans to act; it is the way of things — the nature of the cosmos. Dao as nature contrasts with Dao as a tradition in several aspects. Dao is observed in nature rather than being instructed (spoken of) to pass on a tradition. Everyone has access to learning about the Dao simply by paying close attention to the world around them. A tradition requires qualified instructors who adhere to the official tradition. Qualifications create social hierarchies meant to protect and pass down the tradition in the "right" way. Because the tradition is deemed to be correct, it resists change. If the tradition were to change, then it could not have been correct in the first place. Dao, as nature, invites continual updates as we learn more about the patterns of the cosmos.

This challenge to the stranglehold that tradition poses reminds me of an apocryphal story about Sir. Francis Bacon (1561 - 1626 CE) in Western philosophical development. Sir Francis Bacon rode into town one day. As he approached the market square, a small crowd had gathered. Scholars in heated debate. Bacon, curious, dismounted and listened. The men were arguing about how many teeth a horse has?

One scholar claimed that Aristotle had the answer and launched into a quotation from memory. Another cited a passage from Galen, confident that the truth lay in the classical texts. A third insisted that the theologians had weighed in centuries before and that Scripture left no room for doubt. Their voices rose with certainty.

Bacon, amused, interjected gently. "Has anyone looked in a horse's mouth?"

The scholars fell silent. For a moment, their eyes met in collective uncertainty. Then, as if embarrassed by the suggestion, they resumed their citations, their allegiance firmly planted in the authority of the ancients. Bacon said nothing more. He merely turned to his horse, placed a hand on its jaw, and counted the teeth himself. (In case you are wondering, an adult horse typically has 36 to 44 teeth, depending on sex and whether certain teeth erupt.)

This simple, seemingly mundane act represented a profound shift in the history of thought. In a single gesture, Bacon illustrated the birth of a new way of knowing: empiricism. Where others argued within the inherited echo chamber of tradition, he walked into the world and asked it directly. This was no longer a matter of memorizing ancient truths; it was the beginning of discovering truth through experience in Western thought.

Bacon would formalize this vision in Novum Organum, calling for a method of inquiry rooted in observation and evidence. The story of the horse's teeth became a parable, repeated by later generations as a rebuke to scholasticism — that medieval devotion to arguing from texts rather than from facts. For Bacon, knowledge must be drawn from nature itself, not merely from the pages of dusty tomes.

In this small episode, we see the dawn of the scientific method. The philosopher did not argue. He did not quote. He counted. And in doing so, he changed the world. The Daodejing argued for the same liberation from tradition in this opening line many centuries before.

. . .

There remains one last word to address in line (1). The Dao of nature is described as the "enduring" Dao.

The Chinese character 常 (cháng) plays a significant role in the Daodejing, often appearing in discussions of the Dao and its qualities. Commonly translated as "eternal," cháng more precisely connotes meanings such as "constant," "enduring," or "regular." It suggests something that persists through change, not necessarily timeless in a metaphysical sense, but ongoing, reliable, and unceasing in its presence.

This distinction matters. Translating cháng as "eternal" can mislead readers into interpreting the Dao in supernatural or absolute metaphysical terms, especially when filtered through Western theological frameworks that associate eternity with a static, unchanging divine being. But the Daodejing offers a more dynamic vision. The Dao is not a static object beyond the world but a generative process within it — endlessly manifesting through cycles of emergence and return, flux and stability. In this context, cháng is better understood as enduring — a pattern or principle that persists across transformation, not outside of it.

Change is the only constant. Everything we experience is in motion: the seasons shift, bodies age, emotions rise and fall, societies evolve, and even the stars are born, live, and die. This isn't just poetic sentiment. It is a description of reality at every scale. Nothing stays the same. Nothing is fixed. All things are caught in the flow of impermanence.

To say that "everything changes" is not merely to note that things alter over time. It is to recognize that nothing exists apart from change. Change is not something that happens to things; instead, change is what things are. Looking closely, we see that what we call a "thing" — a tree, a person, a thought — is not a static object but a process. The tree is not a static object with bark and leaves attached. It is a flowing pattern of nutrients, water, light, and genetic unfolding — growing, aging, dropping seeds, and eventually decaying. It is its own transformation.

This process view of reality challenges the way we typically think about existence. Our language tends to freeze the world into nouns — into things. But the more profound truth is that all things are events in motion, momentary configurations of energy, time, and relationship. From this perspective, what appears solid and enduring is actually a temporary coherence, a ripple in the stream, not a rock beneath it. What we call stability is only a pattern that has persisted for now.

The concept of impermanence encourages us not to resist change but to move with it — to develop a kind of flexibility or yielding that allows us to remain in harmony with the world as it unfolds. Clinging to permanence where none exists only causes suffering. However, recognizing that everything is a process — including ourselves — opens up the possibility of a more profound presence, adaptability, and peace.

Now that we have explored the details behind this deceptively simple opening sentence of the Daodejing let me offer a paraphrase of line (1) to help bring out its meaning:

> *A Dao that can be followed (as a tradition) is not*
> *the enduring Dao (of nature).*

Line (2)

The second line shares the same format as the first. A literal translation will illustrate the pattern:

> *dao can dao not enduring dao*
> *name can name not enduring name*

The structure of these two lines is significant. What is said of dao in line (1) is also said of name in line (2). The key to line (1) is to see the contrast between the concepts of Dao as a tradition and Dao of nature. If we add that to the literal translation, we get:

> *dao can dao(tradition) not constant dao(nature)*
> *name can name(tradition) not constant*
> *name(nature)*

We need to understand how the concept of name is connected to tradition and nature. Let's start by reflecting on what a name is.

The concept of a name sits at the heart of human language and social life. To name something is to draw it into shared awareness — to give it a form that can be spoken of, remembered, and acted upon. Names are social tools; they allow us to coordinate, communicate, and cooperate. Without names, we could not pass on knowledge, form agreements, or construct the shared symbolic worlds that make culture possible. To name is to participate in the collective effort of meaning-making — a way of pointing to something and saying, "This is what I mean."

But naming comes with a cost. A name doesn't just point; it fixes. To name something is to carve it out from the flow of experience and treat it as a separate, stable object. In doing so, we risk objectifying what is, in reality, an interconnected process. A river is not the same from one moment to the next — water flows, sediments shift, banks erode and reform — but the word "river" makes it seem like a discrete, unchanging thing. The name hides the movement. The process becomes a thing.

Moreover, naming is also categorizing, and categories flatten differences. No two trees are exactly alike, yet we call them all "trees." In doing so, we overlook each particularity — the specific bark texture, the subtle leaf shape, and the unique place in the forest's ecology. Naming allows us to think efficiently but also encourages us to generalize, substituting the label for the living thing itself. What is unique becomes generic.

The dictum "words are maps, not the territory" captures a crucial insight into the nature of language. A map is a simplified representation of a landscape — it highlights certain features and omits others to serve a specific purpose. Similarly, words do not contain or replicate reality; they point toward it. When we name something — a mountain, a feeling, a person — we create a symbolic marker that allows us to reference that phenomenon in thought and conversation. But just as a map is not the land itself, a word is not the thing it refers to. It is an abstraction layered over the fullness of lived experience.

This becomes especially important to remember so we don't mistake the name for the thing. Once labeled, a phenomenon can become fixed in our minds. The richness of a situation collapses into the shorthand of its description. The name becomes a conceptual filter — it selects certain aspects as meaningful while discarding others as irrelevant. In doing so, words can shape perception itself. We no longer see the event, person, or object in its entire presence; we see our idea of it. In this way, language is both a tool for meaning and a veil over immediacy.

Yet, despite these limitations, we cannot do without names. Human beings are linguistic creatures; our ability to share knowledge, coordinate actions, and build social worlds depends on the power of naming. Language enables everything from scientific discovery to emotional intimacy. The key is not to reject names but to use them wisely — to hold them lightly. We must remember that names are labels placed on top of reality, not reality itself. When we treat them as temporary guides rather than absolute truths, they become tools of clarity rather than instruments of confusion. This humility toward language — this awareness that every word is a map, not the territory — opens the door to a more honest and adaptive relationship with the world.

One of the most significant concerns in early Confucian thought is the concept of rectifying names (正名, zhèng míng), which holds that social order depends on ensuring that words accurately reflect roles, relationships, and responsibilities. For Confucius, language was not simply a means of communication — it was the backbone of moral and political life. When names are used improperly, society's relationships begin to unravel. If a ruler is not acting as a ruler or a father is not acting like a father, yet those titles are still used, confusion arises about what those roles entail. In Confucius' view, this linguistic ambiguity leads to moral and civic disorder.

> Confucius replied, "To govern means to rectify. If
> you lead on the people with correctness, who
> will dare not to be correct?"
> (Analects 12:17, Legge)

At its core, rectifying names is about aligning words with reality, specifically, the reality of proper conduct according to established roles. The "rectification" of names ensures that terms such as "ruler," "minister," "father," and "son" are not just empty labels but carry with them a clearly understood set of duties, expectations, and virtues. To speak rightly is to act rightly. Thus, proper use of names becomes a moral practice that binds individuals to the inherited tradition of ritual and ethical behavior. This is directly tied to Confucius' concept of Dao as the correct tradition — a socially embedded path passed down from the sages of the early Zhou dynasty that must be preserved through correct naming, conduct, and ritual.

In this sense, rectifying names is a conservative strategy: it safeguards the moral order by maintaining the integrity of language. Confucius feared that if the meanings of names were allowed to drift — if people used titles without embodying the virtues those titles implied — society would slide into disorder. Moral decay, for Confucius, begins with linguistic decay. This is why Dao, in his framework, is not a cosmic process (as in the Daodejing) but the way of the sages — a cultivated path of meaning, coherence, and continuity that must be preserved through precise language and proper social roles.

This perspective reveals the close relationship between language, tradition, and ethics in Confucianism. To preserve the Dao is not merely to obey external rules but to speak and act in ways that reflect and reinforce a shared moral vision. In contrast to the Daoist suspicion of naming as a conceptual trap, the Confucian sees correct naming as essential to cultivating virtue and sustaining civilization.

Unlike Confucius' emphasis on rectifying names, Daoist thinkers — especially Zhuangzi — were deeply skeptical that language could reliably track reality or sustain moral order. Where Confucius saw precise naming as essential to preserving the Dao, Zhuangzi saw it as a potential obstacle to genuine understanding. For Daoists, names fix boundaries and distinctions that are, in fact, fluid and interconnected. The world is in constant flux, and carving it up into rigid categories — ruler and subject, good and bad, useful and useless — is both artificial and misleading. Zhuangzi often employs paradox, humor, and storytelling to dissolve fixed distinctions, illustrating how names can confine us to partial perspectives and blind us to the ever-changing, relational nature of the Dao. Instead of rectifying names, the Daoist response is to loosen the grip of names altogether, to return to a kind of primal receptivity where things are allowed to be as they are, unencumbered by conceptual labels. In this way, Daoists do not reject language entirely. Still, they resist mistaking language for reality and warn against building moral or social systems on the unstable foundation of rigid linguistic categories. Note how Zhuangzi remarks on the balance between the use of words and the reality behind them in Chapter 26 of the Zhuangzi:

> The fish trap exists because of the fish; once
>   you've gotten the fish, you can forget the
>   trap. The rabbit snare exists because of the
>   rabbit; once you've gotten the rabbit, you can
>   forget the snare. Words exist because of
>   meaning; once you've gotten the meaning,
>   you can forget the words. Where can I find a
>   man who has forgotten words so I can have a
>   word with him?
> (Watson)

In Confucian thought, the Dao is fundamentally a moral tradition — a path of right conduct cultivated through the refinement of rituals, roles, and virtues. In this framework, names carry normative weight. They are not merely descriptive labels but value-laden designations that tell people how to behave. To call someone a "father," a "minister," or a "ruler" is to invoke a set of ethical expectations. Each name is a social role tied to a moral standard rooted in the sages of antiquity. The process of zhèng míng — rectifying names — aims to ensure that these titles are not misused. Names must match behavior; otherwise, social harmony collapses. Here, names prescribe how things ought to be.

In contrast, the Daodejing views the Dao not as a human tradition but as a cosmic process: the natural unfolding of the world in its own rhythms and transformations. In this view, names are attempts to describe, not prescribe. They are tools for pointing at aspects of an interconnected and ever-changing reality. It cautions that names are limited — they simplify, isolate, and often distort the deeper complexity of the world. To name something means to separate it from the whole and treat it as a distinct object rather than a dynamic process. For Daoists, the concern is not whether names are morally proper but whether they obscure the flowing nature of reality.

Thus, where Confucian naming is normative — concerned with upholding the right values and behaviors — in the Daodejing, naming is skeptical and provisional, aware that names describe only fragments and never the whole. The Confucian dao is maintained through the precise use of morally charged names; the comic Dao is approached by letting go of names to attune more directly to the unfolding of nature itself. In this way, the contrast reflects a more profound philosophical divide: one seeks order through moral clarity, and the other seeks harmony through receptive awareness.

· · ·

We can see now that line (2) does not reinforce the idea that the Dao cannot be spoken of; instead, it reinforces the idea that a traditional Dao is not the Dao of nature.

Here is a paraphrase of the opening two lines that highlights the distinction being made between a Dao of tradition and a Dao of nature:

> *A Dao that can be followed (as a tradition) is not*
> *the enduring Dao (of nature).*
> *Names (of traditional values - prescriptive) can*
> *name no enduring (natural) name*
> *(descriptive - because there are no values in*
> *nature).*

A great deal is packed into the first two lines of the Daodejing. With not-so-quiet force, the text opens with a disruption — a direct challenge to the dominant philosophical outlook of its time and, arguably, of ours as well. It strikes at the heart of any system that pretends to fully define, control, or enclose reality with language or doctrine. In doing so, the Daodejing positions itself against the dogmatic traditions — both ancient and modern — that insist on a single, correct worldview, vocabulary, and path.

This challenge remains remarkably relevant today. We live in a world where philosophical, political, and ideological factions compete for influence and narrative dominance. These systems are not content to describe the world — they seek to name it authoritatively, fix its meaning, and demand compliance. But in doing so, they often distort reality, reducing its complexity to convenient categories and pushing rigid interpretations that fail to account for life's fluid, interdependent nature. How many of our current crises — social, ecological, or existential — are fueled by clinging to frameworks that no longer reflect the changing conditions of our world?

The Daodejing offers an alternative. Rather than replacing one dogma with another, it invites us to adopt a posture of openness and attunement. The remainder of this chapter in the Daodejing will provide us with powerful tools for seeing more clearly, loosening our grip on inherited assumptions, and navigating the world with humility and responsiveness. It offers a methodology of seeing that may help us engage with the challenges of modern life with greater clarity, creativity, and compassion.

The fundamental issue I see here is that if the nature of reality is constant change, a tradition that claims to be correct will always fail to correspond to reality because the nature of the tradition is static, striving not to change.

Lines (3) and (4)

But is it the case that the nature of reality is constant change? The following two lines explore change by introducing the concepts of absence and presence.

> 3. *Absence names the origin of heaven and earth.*
> 4. *Presence names the mother of the ten*
>   *thousand things.*

Before addressing the particulars of absence and

presence, I want to look at the balance of these two lines. First, we see the use of names to describe two aspects of the cosmic Dao, absence and presence. As the chapter progresses, we will see that even though we have given two different names for these concepts, they are not separate. Names are not the ultimate reality; they are useful labels we apply on top of reality to help us understand the Way of things, the Dao. This further illustrates the Daoists' suspicion of using names. Names are necessary to communicate but don't mistake them for the experienced reality behind the words.

The names of both absence and presence attempt to describe a process. In this case, the origin and the mother are both generative acts. Note that this process of the Dao is personified as female.

In the Daodejing, the word 天 (tiān) is often translated as "heaven." However, this term can be misleading if taken in a theological or supernatural sense. Unlike in many Western traditions where "Heaven" suggests a transcendent deity or a realm of divine judgment, the concept of tiān in the thought of the Daodejing reflects a far more naturalistic and impersonal order — one that is embedded within the processes of the world itself rather than standing above or apart from them.

In the context of the Daodejing, 天 (tiān) refers to the overarching order of the cosmos — the patterns and forces that govern the skies, the seasons, the rhythms of time, and, by extension, the unfolding of all life. It is often paired with

地 (dì), "earth," to form the compound 天地 (tiāndì), or "heaven and earth." This phrase is a shorthand for all of nature or the entire cosmos.

Importantly, 天 is not moralistic or providential in the Daoist worldview. It neither rewards virtue nor punishes wrongdoing. Tiān operates without sentimentality, preference, or intervention. It follows the Dao — the spontaneous unfolding of things — and it does so without intention or will. In this sense, tiān models the kind of non-coercive, non-anxious action that sages aspire to emulate in the Daodejing.

By contrast, when we see the term 天下 (tiānxià), literally "under heaven," we are no longer referring to the cosmos in general but to the realm of human society — the world as organized by political systems, social customs, and cultural activity. Tiānxià refers to "the world" as humans experience and attempt to govern it. It appears in the Daodejing in discussions about leadership, harmony, and rulership, often pointing out the disturbance caused when human ambition disrupts the natural balance. To govern tiānxià well, one must align with the rhythms of tiāndì, not oppose them.

What emerges from this linguistic structure is a layered vision of reality. At the broadest level, heaven and earth (tiāndì) encompass the totality of natural processes. Within that more extensive system, the world under heaven (tiānxià) represents the human domain, not separate from nature, but a subset of it. The Daoist perspective emphasizes that any human order worth sustaining must be grounded in an awareness of the greater order of nature. When human activity (tiānxià) loses sight of the broader unfolding of tiāndì, imbalance and suffering follow.

In this way, the Daodejing presents a naturalist vision of heaven — not a place nor a personified god, but a term for the regularities of the universe, the skyward processes, and the cycles of climate and time. To live in harmony with heaven, then, is to learn to move in rhythm with the larger world — to trust the patterns that sustain life and to act with the humility of knowing that we are not above nature but entirely within it.

As we continue, let us pause and recall the earlier section, Attending to Absence and Presence, where we explored the fundamental rhythm of reality described in the Daodejing. In that section, we saw how absence (無 wú) refers not to nothingness but to formlessness — the open, unseen potential from which things arise. Presence (有 yǒu) is the moment of form when something takes shape and becomes visible, tangible, and nameable. But presence is never permanent; what has form eventually dissolves. What arises returns. This ongoing transformation — from absence to presence and back again — is the very pattern of the Dao itself. It is through this endless movement that the world unfolds, sustains itself, and renews.

What begins to take shape in the Daodejing is an image of reality that is not built on static objects or isolated entities but on patterns of movement, emergence, and return. The world is not made of things in the conventional sense but of transformations — of appearances arising from formlessness and dissolving back into it. The Dao is not behind or beyond this process but inherent within it: the unfolding of things according to their own nature, the rhythm by which everything participates in a larger whole.

This pattern — from absence to presence and back again — gives rise to a vision of interrelatedness. Nothing exists independently. Every form is shaped by its context, every moment by what precedes and follows it. Even what seems distinct and self-contained is inseparable from what surrounds and sustains it. Your body seems distinct and self-contained, but can it be separated from air, earth, water, and food? The boundaries we perceive are temporary, drawn by perception and naming, not by the world itself. From this perspective, difference is real, but it is not ultimate. All things, arising and returning, share a common origin and destiny.

This view naturally leads to the concept of oneness, not a sameness that erases differences but a recognition that all things participate in a single, dynamic process. Oneness is not a belief but a perception: a shift in how we see the world, no longer as a collection of separate entities but as a flowing pattern with many faces. To live in accordance with the Dao is to recognize this oneness, to move with it rather than against it, and to see in every presence the silent trace of absence and the echo of emergence in every return. This is not unity imposed from above but a harmony discovered within — a quiet coherence that reveals itself only to those willing to look beyond the surface and into the source.

· · ·

Lines (5), (6), and (7)

After confronting a radically integrated view of reality, the chapter turns to a strategy for observing our world. How we focus our awareness reveals different nuances. Our goal is to see how these differences are unified despite having unique names.

> 5. *Focus on enduring absence by observing its*
>   *mystery,*
> 6. *Focus on enduring presence by observing its*
>   *manifestations,*
> 7. *[Until] both are unified (although they differ*
>   *in name).*

In lines (5) and (6), the Chinese character translated as "observing" is guān (觀). Guān is a Classical Chinese verb that generally means to observe, watch, or contemplate. It suggests more than casual looking; it implies a focused, attentive kind of seeing, often with the goal of insight or understanding. The character is composed of two characters: 見 (jiàn), "to see," and 雚 (guàn), originally a bird used in ancient sacrificial rituals, which contributes to the sense of sacred or elevated (bird's eye) observation. Historically, guān was also used for temples or towers of observation (e.g., an astronomical observatory), reinforcing the sense of elevated, distanced seeing, seeing with perspective.

I begin with my thoughts on observing to help make sense of my unusual translation of yù as "focus." 欲 (yù) is often translated as "desire" in the conventional sense — an attachment to things, labels, or distinctions. Yù can also be understood more broadly as any directed attention, fixation, or conceptual framing. To interpret yù as "focus" is not to deny its core meaning of desire but to see desire as a kind of cognitive constriction — a narrowing of awareness that affects what we see and how we relate to the world.

If yù is translated as desire, then the absence or presence of desire changes what we see. However, it is not merely "seeing" that these lines suggest. Instead, observing and contemplating carefully allows us to perceive the mystery and the manifestations. Neither of these observations is identified as better than the other. Both are valid ways of seeing, just from different angles. Absence and presence, mystery and manifestations, are both part of reality, both part of the Dao. My translation of yù as "focus" rather than "desire" helps to bring out this understanding. Perhaps more importantly, this translation also preserves absence and presence as the continued topic.

The active nature of contemplating through observing the mysteries of absence and the manifestations of presence leads me to see line (7) as a goal of the observation rather than merely a statement about the unity of the two. The importance of using the names (line (2)) of absence and presence in lines (3) and (4) is to help us perceive what is usually hidden. That absence is not nothing (no-thing). Absence names the generative source of presence. And presence names everything we perceive. Then, lines (5) and (6) call us to reflect on these two patterns until, in line (7), we can understand enduring absence and enduring presence as part of the one enduring Dao of line (1). And to realize that the use of the different names is only a helpful tool, a label that separates what is actually a unity.

Lines (8), (9), and (10)

The chapter takes an interesting turn at this point, referring to the unity of absence and presence, mystery and manifestation, as darkness.

> *8. Call this unity darkness,*
> *9. Darkness within darkness,*
> *10. The entrance to all mysteries.*

In Western cultural and philosophical traditions, the concept of "darkness" often carries negative connotations. It is commonly associated with ignorance, evil, danger, confusion, and death — a space of the unknown to be feared or overcome. From biblical imagery, where darkness symbolizes sin or separation from divine light, to Enlightenment-era metaphors that frame knowledge as "light" dispelling the "darkness" of superstition, the symbolic contrast between light and dark has been used to enforce a moral and intellectual hierarchy. In literature and popular culture, darkness frequently denotes a threat — a setting for villainy, moral decay, or psychological disturbance. In Western contexts, these associations are so deeply embedded that it becomes challenging to see darkness as fertile, generative, or essential — qualities associated with darkness in the context of yinyang.

In the context of yinyang philosophy and the Daodejing,

the word "darkness" is a vital, nurturing, and integral aspect of reality. It represents the hidden, the receptive, the fertile, the restful — the complementary counterpart to light, not its enemy. The mystery of the Dao is described here as emerging from "darkness within darkness," a phrase that points to the depth of the ungraspable — the origin of all things that cannot be seen or named. In this worldview, darkness is the source, not the absence of value. It is the space in which life begins, like the womb or the soil. Rather than something to fear or eliminate, darkness is something to enter, trust, and attune to, especially when seeking the subtle and enduring patterns of the Dao. This perspective invites a different kind of awareness that honors stillness over action, depth over clarity, and the unseen over the obvious, restoring darkness to its rightful place as half of a dynamic, generative whole.

In the Daodejing, the association of yin with the female is not merely a cultural metaphor but a deep reflection of how Daoist thought understands the world's generative, receptive, and transformative power. We read in lines (3) and (4):

> 3. *Absence names the origin of heaven and earth.*
> 4. *Presence names the mother of the ten*
>   *thousand things.*

Here, absence, the formlessness potential, gives rise to the cosmos (heaven and earth). Presence, the formed, is called the mother of all things. This mother metaphor grounds the Dao's yin aspect in creativity, emergence, and care, not weakness or subordination. The mother does not create by force but by allowing and making space for life to unfold in its own way. She does not impose form but makes form possible by providing the conditions for gestation and growth.

In Daoist cosmology, yin is the mode of novelty and transformation. It is associated with darkness, stillness, and the unseen; these qualities are fertile. Just as seeds sprout in the dark soil and infants grow in the hidden depths of the womb, creation arises from what is not yet visible. Yin is thus the source of newness — the place where the ten thousand things emerge before they take on distinct forms.

This perspective reframes the idea of femininity from a Daoist standpoint: as a cosmic principle of creativity and continuity. The Daodejing frequently uses the image of the mother and, later, the valley spirit (谷神) to evoke the inexhaustible and ungraspable source from which all things arise. This maternal metaphor elevates the yin principle as the deep strength of life itself, not in opposition to yang, but as the ground of its possibility. From this silent, open, and undirected space, novelty comes into being as the natural unfolding of the Dao.

One compelling critique found within the Daodejing, especially when viewed against the backdrop of the Warring States period, is that the social and political chaos of the time was in large part the result of an overemphasis on yang — that is, an excess of assertive, hierarchical, and controlling modes of action commonly associated with masculine authority, rigid roles, militarism, and rational order. The world had become controlled by systems of domination: rulers enforcing strict rituals, ministers engaging in competition for status, and states waging endless wars to assert power and maintain order. In such an environment, yang values — clarity, control, conquest, and assertion — had come to dominate governance and philosophical discourse, including that of Confucianism and Legalism, which emphasized moral correctness, structured social roles, and prescriptive behavior.

The Daodejing can be read as a strategic reassertion of yin in response to this imbalance. Rather than meeting force with force or rigidity with more structure, it advocates for a return to what is soft, yielding, receptive, and unassuming. Yin, in this sense, is not a weakness but a different kind of strength that emerges from adaptability, openness, and alignment with the world's natural rhythms. Throughout the text, water is praised for its softness and humility, yet it erodes rock. The female, the valley, and the infant are held up as symbols of power precisely because they do not strive or impose.

In this reading, the Daodejing is not simply mystical poetry or quietist retreat but a subtle political intervention. It critiques the dominant order by exposing its brittleness and detachment from the more profound life processes. The answer to social disintegration is not more rules, control, or rigid morality but a rebalancing — a return to humility, softness, patience, and silence. By elevating yin, the Daodejing presents an alternative model of power, one grounded in non-coercion, relational attunement, and the wisdom of yielding — a radical vision, especially in a time of fragmentation and war.

Darkness is not merely a lack of light but a profound symbol for the threshold of insight — the entrance to understanding the unity of absence and presence. This poetic phrase suggests a way of seeing that doesn't rely on clear definitions, but on being open to things we can't easily understand. In the Daoist view, it is precisely through entering this darkness — the space of the unseen, the unformed, the unnamed — that one begins to sense the interdependence of absence and presence, of what is and what is not. Darkness becomes the place of convergence, where the visible and invisible, form and formlessness, arise together and return. Approaching this mystery requires not more analysis but a loosening of conceptual distinctions — a quieting of the impulse to name and fix. In this way, darkness is not the absence of knowledge but the condition for a more profound, holistic knowing that feels its way into the unity behind all differentiation.

SUMMARY OF CHAPTER ONE OF THE DAODEJING

The opening chapter is a masterful overture to the Daodejing. In a few poetic words, the author presents the primary argument, justifies it, and introduces the reader to many of the key themes that will be explored throughout the rest of the book. Lines (1) and (2) make the case for a unique understanding of what is meant by "Dao" in sharp contrast to the dominant view of the day. Rather than defining Dao as a tradition or a social contract to be followed, Dao is here identified as the cosmic Dao, or the Way of the universe. Lines (3) and (4) present a view of the nature of reality as absence and presence that supports the opening position of a comic Dao. Then, lines (5), (6), and (7) present us with strategies for how we perceive the world based on the cosmic Dao perspective. Lastly, lines (8), (9), and (10) offer a disposition to adopt that is more in alignment with a cosmic understanding of Dao.

CHAPTER 5

EMBODIED DAO

U p to this point, we've explored the worldview of the Daodejing — a way of seeing grounded in relationship, impermanence, and dynamic balance. However, the Dao is not a concept to be mastered. It is not an idea to believe in. It is a way to walk, a way to live. The goal is not just to understand the pattern intellectually but to begin living within it consciously — to shift how we attend, interpret, and engage with the world.

In the following pages, we'll explore how to begin embodying the insights we've covered so far. The following reflections are not instructions in the usual sense. They are invitations — ways to redirect your attention, soften your stance, and realign your life with the unfolding pattern of the Dao.

1. Everything is Connected

Nothing stands alone. You do not arise alone, move alone, or act alone. The Daodejing presents a world in which everything co-arises — not separate things bumping into each other, but dynamic patterns flowing through one another. To live this insight is to begin noticing how every aspect of your life is intricately connected in relationships.

Pause and ask:

- What invisible support systems make my life possible today?
- Who or what am I responding to right now?
- How would I speak or act differently if I genuinely felt the web I'm part of?

As you move through your day, keep the quiet awareness that you are not at the center of things but at a point of convergence. You are where the pattern becomes visible. Let this change how you listen, move, and care.

2. Attending to Absence and Presence

What you see is only part of what's there. Presence is always resting on absence. The cup holds tea because it is hollow. A conversation makes sense because of its pauses. The Daodejing returns again and again to the usefulness of what is not there — the empty space, the silence, the unformed.

.   .   .

Practice noticing:

- What is supporting this moment from the background?
- What is not being said that makes what is said meaningful?
- What roles are being played by stillness, delay, or restraint?

Attending to absence does not mean ignoring the visible. It means remembering that form is shaped by formlessness and that both are part of the unfolding pattern. Let go of needing everything to be named, explained, or filled. Learn to rest in the space between.

3. Co-Dependent Origination

Nothing originates on its own. Every moment, every thought, every choice is part of a greater flow of causes and conditions. The Daodejing never speaks of control. It speaks of alignment — with the wind, with the season, with what is already moving.

Reflect on:

- What part of this situation is not about me?
- How might awareness of the whole change how I respond?

- What recent experience or reaction was shaped by conditions I didn't notice?
- What stories do I tell about being "self-made" or "on my own"?
- Can I trace one small action today back to its many causes?

To live from this view is to understand that you are not the source of action — you are the site of interaction. Your insight, presence, and influence arise not in isolation but as expressions of a larger process. To act wisely is to act with the pattern, not against it.

4. Transformation is the Way

Nothing stays the same. The Dao is constantly moving — not in chaos, but in rhythm. What is high will become low. What is strong will become soft. What you fear or long for is already in the process of becoming something else. Transformation is not the exception; it is the way.

Return to this question often:

- What is changing right now?
- What am I trying to preserve that is already shifting?
- What wants to emerge that I've been resisting?

When you see clearly that everything is a process, you

stop clinging to outcomes and begin to trust the rhythm. Let this trust shape your actions. Be like water — responsive, persistent, without form, yet able to take any form.

THE DAO IS NOT FAR AWAY

To embody the Dao is not to withdraw from the world or escape complexity. It is to live more fully within it, with eyes attuned to connection, ears sensitive to silence, and actions that participate rather than impose. This is not a new belief system. It is a new kind of attention. You are not becoming something different. You are becoming more fully aligned with what you already are — a moment of pattern in the unfolding whole.

Let your life begin to feel the rhythm beneath the noise. Let your choices arise from the stillness at the root. Let your way of being become the Way itself.

Two additional forces that support transformation, often overlooked, are mental fixation and shared worldview. When a new insight first takes root, especially one as perspective-altering as the Daoist view of interdependence and process, it can become a mental obsession. This isn't necessarily a problem. Repeated contemplation, turning an idea over from different angles and letting it echo through daily experience, is part of how profound change happens. Just as a stone is smoothed by prolonged exposure to flowing water, our worldview is reshaped through sustained attention. Letting your mind return again and again to the same questions — not to solve them, but to live with them — is a form of inner alignment. Transformation often begins when we stop trying to master an idea and instead let it saturate us.

Equally important is the role of community as relational reinforcement. Worldviews are fragile when held alone. Sharing space, stories, or conversations with others who see the world through similar eyes helps normalize a way of being that the larger culture may ignore or resist. In such a space, the Dao isn't something you have to explain or defend — it becomes something you inhabit together. Even brief interactions can strengthen your commitment to living differently. Community offers mirrors and reminders, a field in which the pattern of the Dao becomes visible between people, not just within them. Transformation, like everything else in Daoist thought, is not solitary — it is a process of co-arising, nourished through shared presence. Check out our community at: www.Kinship.Cafe

Part One has primarily focused on perception, the first and necessary step towards the Way of Kinship. Everything flows from your worldview. From a personal perspective, how we perceive reality is often more impactful than reality itself because our brain doesn't give us a direct feed of the external world — it provides us with a simulation. Neuroscience has shown that the brain is constantly generating predictions about what it expects to happen based on past experiences and then updating those predictions based on incoming sensory data. This process —

often called predictive processing — means that what we consciously experience is not the raw world "out there", but a model created inside our heads, constantly adjusted to match the signals we receive. In this way, perception is not passive reception but active construction.

This has profound consequences for how we live. If you believe the world is hostile, even neutral events will be interpreted as threats. If you see yourself as unworthy, even kindness can feel suspicious. Conversely, if you perceive the world as interconnected, generous, and evolving, you begin to notice support, opportunity, and relationships where others might see only randomness or struggle. The Daodejing offers a worldview — one that, when deeply integrated, reshapes the very nature of the simulation itself. What we perceive is what we live inside. So, when we shift our perception, we don't just see differently — we experience life differently. In this sense, changing your worldview isn't abstract philosophy — it's experiential transformation.

PART TWO
DE 德

CHAPTER 6
LIVING DIFFERENTLY

In the Daodejing, De is best understood as the natural, spontaneous expression of the Dao in individual beings. While Dao is the underlying source and pattern of the cosmos, the Way, De, is the specific way in which the Way becomes embodied and visible in particular forms. It is often translated as "virtue," "power," or "integrity," but these English terms only partially capture its meaning. In the Daodejing, De is not about moral righteousness; it is about inner potency, authentic character, and the natural excellence of things aligned with the Dao. In Part Two, we will examine how our updated worldview, our perception of the world through the lens of the Dao (Part One), influences how we live out The Way of Kinship in our day-to-day lives (De).

DE (德)

The character 德 (dé) is composed of meaningful components that help reveal its significance in the Daoist tradition. On the left is the radical 彳 (chì), which means "step" or "to go," suggesting movement or conduct. On the right are three parts: 直 (zhí), meaning "upright" or "straight," 心 (xīn), the heart-mind, and 目 (mù), the eye. Together, these components evoke the image of a person who moves through the world with upright clarity, guided by heart and vision. 德 , then, is not simply moral correctness; it is the embodied expression of alignment with the Dao — a kind of cultivated integrity or natural potency that arises when one acts with internal coherence, awareness, and responsiveness. It reflects how one's way of being radiates outward through presence grounded in the rhythm of the greater pattern.

When a person, an animal, a tree, or even a river follows its natural course without forcing or distorting itself, it manifests De. In human terms, De arises when someone acts without pretension or excessive interference, when they live simply, humbly, and fluidly, allowing their nature to unfold in harmony with the greater Dao.

Importantly, De is deeply relational. It is not a static inner quality but a living expression of how one moves within the shifting patterns of the world. It is the "rightness" of being in accord with the hidden rhythms of life rather than imposing fixed standards or rigid rules. This quiet, effortless power comes from deep alignment rather than self-assertion.

In Confucian philosophy, De refers to cultivated moral character — the internalization of virtue achieved through education, ritual, and adherence to tradition. It is both personal and social: a person's De shapes not only their own behavior but also their influence on others, especially in the role of a ruler or moral exemplar. For Confucius, De is built upon a conscious effort to align oneself with the values of the past sages, such as kindness (仁 rén), righteousness (義 yì), and ritual (禮 lǐ). A person of strong De leads by moral example rather than by force, creating harmony through their presence. In this view, De is inseparable from social roles and ethical norms — it is a moral force cultivated within the framework of a well-ordered society.

In contrast, the Daodejing presents De not as a moral achievement but as natural potency — the unforced expression of the Dao within and through things. Daoist De does not come from learning or conforming to tradition but from yielding to the patterns of the cosmos and acting without contrivance (無 為 wúwéi). It is spontaneous, unselfconscious, and beyond praise or blame. Where Confucian De seeks to refine the self to fulfill a social role, Daoist De arises when the self steps back, allowing the Dao to act through it. In Daoism, De is a kind of integrity without an agenda, not a virtue to be cultivated, but rather a resonance with the natural unfolding of reality.

DAODEJING (道德經)

With the definition of Dao and De, we can now explain the book's title. The final Chinese character in the title is Jing

(經 jīng). Jing, often translated as "classic," "scripture," or "canon," originally means "warp" (as in the vertical threads of woven fabric) and conveys the idea of something enduring, foundational, and guiding — a text or teaching that serves as a structural principle for life and society, much like warp threads provide the structure for a piece of cloth. Calling the work a jing suggests that it contains fundamental truths or enduring wisdom intended to serve as a guide across generations.

So, the title Daodejing can be translated as The Book of Dao and its Manifestations. However, the book was initially known as The Laozi after the supposed author. Several centuries later, during the Han dynasty, texts were increasingly formalized under names that reflected their philosophical content. Naming it Daodejing helped distinguish it as a classic philosophical work, on par with other "jing" texts, such as the Yijing (Classic of Changes, also written as I Ching).

LAOZI (老子)

Laozi is the legendary author traditionally credited with writing the Daodejing. His biographical details are vague, and most historians consider him a mythical or semi-mythical figure. According to Sima Qian's Records of the Grand Historian (c. 1st century BCE), Laozi was a record keeper in the Zhou dynasty's archives. Disillusioned with the world's corruption, he left civilization riding a water buffalo toward the West. At the western gate, a guardian asked him to leave behind his wisdom, and Laozi composed the Daodejing — a text of about 5,000 characters — before disappearing into the unknown.

The meaning of the name "Laozi" literally means "Old Master" or "Venerable Teacher." I like Komjathy's observation that this can be a plural term meaning "The Venerable Masters" (Komjathy, 2023, 4).

WUWEI (無為)

In the Daodejing, 無為 (wúwéi) is often translated as "non-action" or "effortless action," but these translations can easily be misunderstood. It does not mean doing nothing, passivity, or indifference. Rather, wuwei points to a natural, spontaneous, and uncontrived way of acting — an action that arises in harmony with the unfolding of the Dao, free from artificial striving or socially imposed constructions.

The phrase 無為 (wúwéi) is composed of two characters: 無 (wú), meaning "without" or "non-," and 為 (wéi), which generally means "action," "doing," or "effort." On the surface, the phrase can be read as "without action," but in the context of the Daodejing, it takes on a more nuanced, technical meaning. Here, 為 (wéi) does not refer to all forms of action but specifically to intentional, contrived, or socially constructed forms of action — those shaped by external norms, moral ideals, or cultural expectations. Thus, wuwei points to a way of being that acts without forcing, without artificiality, and without conforming to imposed standards — primarily the actions shaped by social expectations, ambitions, rigid hierarchies, and fabricated identities.

Consider how beauty standards influence the behavior of many women. From a young age, they are told — explicitly and implicitly — what they "should" look like: a particular body type, skin tone, hairstyle, or style of dress. These standards are not natural truths but socially constructed ideals, reinforced by advertising, media, and cultural norms. As a result, a woman may spend hours applying makeup she doesn't enjoy, wearing clothes that feel uncomfortable, or even undergoing painful procedures — not because these actions arise naturally from her sense of self, but because they are performed to meet external expectations.

Wuwei offers another way: rather than forcing herself into those contrived molds, she could act from a place of authenticity — choosing how to present herself based on comfort, creativity, or genuine self-expression, free from the pressure to conform to someone else's idea of beauty. Wuwei doesn't mean rejecting all grooming or style but letting go of the forcing that comes from chasing approval. In doing so, her actions become less about performing an identity and more about being. It may feel like we don't have an option to be more genuinely ourselves in our world, and that is part of the point. Here we are only exposing the concept; the solution will have to be worked out as we learn more about the contrasting worldviews that are generating this dilemma. A key insight of Daodejing is that personal well-being cannot be separated from social and political institutions.

In the context of the Warring States period, where ritual, moralistic codes, and political manipulation dominated society, the Daodejing suggests that most human behavior had become inauthentic and layered with pretense and ambition. People were no longer moving naturally with life; they were performing roles, following scripts invented by culture rather than by nature.

Wuwei is a return to acting without the weight of these layers. It is to respond to life fluidly, like water finding its way through a landscape, without clinging to a fixed idea of what one "should" do according to custom, pride, or fear. It is about allowing one's actions to emerge from the immediate conditions of life, guided by sensitivity to the larger patterns of change rather than from rigid codes or ego-driven plans. In this sense, wuwei is a liberation from socially constructed ways of acting, a return to primal responsiveness that is more effective, sustainable, and in tune with the reality of constant change.

The sage who practices wuwei is not inactive; they are deeply engaged with the world. But they act without forcing, without competing unnecessarily, and without trying to control outcomes. Their leadership or influence emerges naturally, much like a valley nurturing life without effort or water nourishing without striving. It is a mode of being that trusts the intelligence of life itself rather than imposing artificial structures onto it.

Here are a few real-world examples that illustrate wuwei as non-artificial, spontaneous, responsive action rather than inaction:

1. In Art: The Calligrapher or Musician

A master calligrapher does not consciously plan each brushstroke. Instead, after years of practice, the hand moves naturally, without overthinking, responding fluidly to the brush, the ink, and the moment. Similarly, a skilled jazz musician improvises effortlessly, listening deeply to the other players and the emerging music rather than trying to dominate or rigidly control the performance. This is wuwei — action arising from deep attunement, without contrivance or self-conscious striving.

2. In Leadership: The Invisible Leader

A great leader practicing wuwei does not constantly issue commands or micro-manage. Instead, they create the right conditions — clear vision, trust, empowerment — so that people act effectively and independently. As the Daodejing says, the best leaders are those whose influence is so natural that when success is achieved, the people say, "We did it ourselves" (Chapter 17). The leader does not impose artificial control but subtly shapes the environment, aligning actions with the larger needs of the group.

3. In Personal Life: Parenting with Flexibility

A parent practicing wuwei does not rigidly enforce an idealized vision of what their child must become. Instead, they observe carefully, nurture strengths as they naturally emerge, and adapt their guidance to the child's unfolding character. Rather than forcing a pre-set mold, they respond to actual needs, allowing growth to happen organically and trusting the innate vitality of the child's nature.

4. In Everyday Action: Responding Without Overplanning

In daily life, wuwei can appear as making a decision quickly and clearly because the situation demands it, rather than agonizing over every possible outcome. It can mean trusting intuition grounded in experience rather than becoming paralyzed by second-guessing or external expectations. It is the difference between moving with the current and fighting against it unnecessarily.

In these examples, wuwei is not passivity — it is a kind of active receptivity: a trust in life's unfolding, a willingness to engage without the distortions of excessive control, self-importance, or rigid social constructs. It is a way of living informed by knowledge of the Dao.

In Part One, we went into detail on the first and most important aspect of the Way of Kinship, our perception of the interconnectedness of everything. Living from that perspective necessarily changes how we live. In the language of the Daodejing, once we comprehend the Dao, the inviable way of the universe, we need to bring our actions and way of being into alignment and harmony with the Dao; this is known as De, the manifestation of Dao.

In Part Two of the Way of Kinship, De is the focus. What

does it mean to manifest the Dao, and how do we do that? The traditional chapter that kicks off the De section of the Daodejing is chapter 38, which we will now explore in detail. I begin with the original text and my translation, just as I did for Chapter 1 of the Daodejing. Chapter 38 is a prime example of the cryptic and minimalistic style of writing found in the Daodejing that can initially sound very confusing. The words can be deliberately provocative and hyperbolic. Don't worry, each line will be explored in detail to help bring out the significance of what is said here.

CHAPTER 7

DAODEJING THIRTY-EIGHT

ORIGINAL TEXT

1. 上德不德
shàng dé bù dé

2. 是以有德
shì yǐ yǒu dé

3. 下德不失德
xià dé bù shī dé

4. 是以無德
shì yǐ wú dé

5. 上德無為而無以為
shàng dé wú wéi ér wú yǐ wéi

6. 下德為之而有以為
xià dé wei zhi ér yǒu yǐ wéi

7. 上仁為之而無以為
shàng rén wéi zhī ér wú yǐ wéi

8. 上義為之而有以為
shàng yì wéi zhī ér yǒu yǐ wéi

9. 上禮為之而莫之應
shàng lǐ wéi zhī ér mò zhī yìng

10. 則壞臂而扔之
zé rǎng bì ér rēng zhī

故
gù

11. 失道而後德
shī dào ér hòu dé

12. 失德而後仁
shī dé ér hòu rén

13. 失仁而後義
shī rén ér hòu yì

14. 失義而後禮
shī yì ér hòu lǐ

15. 夫禮者
fú lǐ zhě

16. 忠信之薄而亂之首
zhōng xìn zhī bó ér luàn zhī shǒu

17. 前識者
qián shí zhě

18. 道之華而愚之始
dào zhī huá ér yú zhī shǐ

19. 是以大丈夫
shì yǐ dà zhàng fū

20. 處其厚不居其薄
chǔ qí hòu bù jū qí bó

21. 處其實不居其華
chǔ qí shí bù jū qí huá

22. 故去彼取此
gù qù bǐ qǔ cǐ

TRANSLATION

1. High De not De,

2. Thus, have De.

3. Low De keeps De,

4. Thus, without De.

5. High De does not act on social constructs and is without assumptions.

6. Low De acts on social constructs and has assumptions.

7. High kindness acts on social constructs and is without assumptions.

8. High righteousness acts on social constructs and has assumptions.

9. High ritual acts on social constructs, but when no one responds,

10. Then arms are bared and [compliance] is forced.

This is because:

11. When Dao is forgotten, De arrives.

12. When De is forgotten, kindness arrives.

13. When kindness is forgotten, righteousness arrives.

14. When righteousness is forgotten, ritual arrives.

15. The ritualized self,

16. Is thin on loyalty and truth; confusion leads.

17. One foreknows

18. *[This is perceived as] the flowering of the*
    Dao, but it is the beginning of delusion.
19. *Therefore, a great elder*
20. *Keeps to the thick and not with the thin,*
21. *Keeps to the fruit and not with the flower.*
22. *Thus, let go of that and hold on to this.*

DETAILED COMMENTS

Chapter 38 of the Daodejing is traditionally seen as the transition point that marks the division between the two major sections of the Daodejing: the Dao (道) section, which spans Chapters 1 through 37, and the De (德) section, which begins with Chapter 38. This division is based on the words of the text's title, Daodejing, and reflects a thematic shift. The first half generally focuses on the nature of the Dao: the patterning process that underlies all existence. The second half, beginning with Chapter 38, turns toward De: the manifestation of Dao in human conduct, especially in the realm of governance, ethics, and leadership. Chapter 38 makes this shift explicit by reflecting on the decline from spontaneous natural De to constructed morality, hierarchy, and ritual — a key concern of the Daodejing. In this way, Chapter 38 acts as both a summary of what has come before and a pivot toward how the Dao expresses itself (or is lost) in human behavior and institutions.

Many readers are surprised to find that the Daodejing frequently discusses governance and politics. This may seem at odds with its reputation as a guide for personal wisdom and inner tranquility. But this surprise rests on a misconception: the assumption that people exist as isolated individuals. In the worldview of the Daodejing, nothing exists independently — everything is part of an ongoing web of relationships. Just as a tree depends on soil, sunlight, and rainfall, human well-being is inseparable from the social and political conditions that shape our lives. The text's political reflections are not a detour from its spiritual insights; they are a natural extension of its recognition of interconnectedness.

From this perspective, governing is not merely a technical task or the domain of rulers — it is about tending to the conditions of life in a way that allows people to flourish. When the Daodejing speaks of the ideal ruler or sage, it often points toward principles that are equally applicable in a family, community, or any group dynamic. The goal is not to dominate or control others but to create space for harmony to emerge naturally by avoiding excess, rigidity, and interference. Understanding this broader context helps correct the common assumption that the Daodejing is focused solely on self-cultivation. In Daoism, there is no "self" apart from the field of relationships in which it moves — and so a philosophy of life must also be a philosophy of society.

Lines (1) - (4)

Chapters 1 and 38 share a distinctive feature: each begins with a key term used in two contrasting ways — one rooted in Confucian thought, the other in Daoist philosophy. In Chapter 1, the word Dao is used both in the Confucian sense — as the proper tradition for ordering society — and in the Daoist sense — as the cosmic pattern underlying all things. Similarly, Chapter 38 opens with the word De, which for Confucians refers to the cultivated moral virtue shaped by tradition. At the same time, for Daoists, it represents the spontaneous and natural expression of the Dao in human life. These dual meanings set the stage for the interpretive tension that runs through the text.

1. High De not De,

2. Thus, have De.

3. Low De keeps De,

4. Thus, without De.

In true Daodejing minimalist style, these opening lines present a riddle for the reader to solve. Two concepts of De are contrasted here — one called "high", and the other called "low." Each concept has a strategy and a result. The Confucian concept of De I will label "virtue" — an active process of developing a second nature conforming to a social tradition (the Confucian Dao). The Daoist concept of De I will label "manifestation of Dao." With these labels added to the text, it will help make the wordplay more apparent:

1. High De (manifestation of Dao) not De
    (virtue)

Here, the strategy of high De (the manifestation of Dao) is not to strive to be virtuous. Think of this like carving a stone statue. You cannot add to the stone to create an image; you can only remove the parts that don't belong to reveal the image already present. The parts of the stone that are removed are like socially constructed ways of being that need to be removed so that the natural manifestation of the Dao can be revealed in us. This leads to the result in line (2):

2. Thus, have De (the manifestation of Dao).

In not striving to create De as a virtue, you end up possessing De as the manifestation of Dao. In contrast, there is line (3):

*3. Low De (virtue) keeps [or strives for] De
(virtue)*

The strategy of a virtuous De is to actively strive and cultivate a life of virtue, true to the social tradition. The result is a life of virtue that covers the natural manifestation of Dao:

4. Thus, without De (the manifestation of Dao).

To modern readers, the Daodejing's critique of virtue can sound surprisingly subversive — even shocking. That's because, like Confucianism, much of contemporary culture is grounded in conformity to socially constructed values. We are taught from an early age to be "good," to strive for excellence, and to meet expectations set by family, school, and society — all in ways that mirror the Confucian emphasis on virtue as something to be cultivated through adherence to tradition and social norms. So, when the Daodejing suggests that the highest De does not try to be virtuous or that moral posturing leads to decline, it cuts against deeply internalized assumptions. It challenges the very foundation of how we define what is right and good. In a world saturated with performative morality and identity signaling, the idea that genuine goodness emerges only when we stop trying to "be good" can feel both disorienting and liberating.

Lines (5) - (14)

A central difference between De as virtue and De as the manifestation of the Dao lies in how we determine what is considered right or appropriate. In the Confucian view, De is built on socially constructed values — standards of behavior shaped by tradition and upheld through moral education. In contrast, the Daoist perspective sees De as something that arises naturally, without the need for imposed rules or ideals.

Lines (5) - (6) illustrate how the difference between the two understandings of De shapes how one acts, and the mindset behind the action. Specifically, one's actions are either 為 (wéi) or 無為 (wúwéi) with the mindset of 以為 (yǐwéi) or not. Let me explain.

Recall that earlier, we defined wuwei as acting in life without imposing, striving, or manipulating — it is to trust that right action arises when one is deeply in sync with the patterns of the larger whole. Just as rivers flow, plants grow, and seasons change unforcedly in response to unfolding patterns of nature, wuwei is acting without coercion from socially constructed norms or values. Acting according to wei is just the opposite. Wei, in this technical sense, is striving to have one's actions conform to socially constructed norms or values. The mindset of yiwei involves assumptions, in this case, a mistaken belief in the objectivity of the social constructions.

In the Daodejing, the problem with conforming one's actions to socially constructed norms or values (為 wéi) is that it leads one away from the natural flow of the Dao. When behavior is shaped by external ideals — such as conventional notions of beauty, goodness, or propriety — it becomes artificial, performative, and disconnected from the deep patterns of the world. The text repeatedly warns that when people act according to these constructed values, they lose touch with the spontaneous wisdom that arises from being attuned to the Dao.

The Daodejing views this reliance on socially constructed values as the precursor to ethical and social decline. Once people start trying to be good, just, or virtuous in ways that conform to set ideals, they introduce hierarchy, competition, and hypocrisy. Rather than cultivating harmony, these efforts generate division between what is accepted and what is rejected, between those deemed worthy and those deemed unworthy. This kind of action (為) is rooted in willful striving and judgment, which disrupts the effortless balance that wuwei seeks to maintain. In Daoism, the ideal is to act without force, allowing things to unfold in accordance with their nature. Conforming to socially constructed norms severs this alignment, placing human effort above the natural order — a move that, according to the Daodejing, ultimately leads to disorder and suffering.

. . .

A clear example can be seen in the era of alcohol prohibition in the United States (1920–1933). Prohibition was driven by a moral ideal: that banning alcohol would eliminate vice, strengthen families, and elevate public morality. Religious groups, temperance activists, and reform-minded politicians believed that forcing people to be "good" by eliminating access to alcohol would create a more virtuous society. Prohibition is a textbook case of action rooted in 為 (wéi) — deliberate, ideal-driven interference with the natural flow of life.

From a Daoist perspective, this effort exemplifies the kind of rigid moral intervention that disrupts harmony rather than cultivating it. By trying to impose virtue from the top down, prohibition introduced division between "law-abiding citizens" and "criminals," created a thriving black market, fueled organized crime, and eroded respect for law and government. Rather than solving social ills, it amplified them.

Prohibition exemplifies how forcing virtue through artificial structures leads to unintended consequences. Instead of addressing the root causes of alcohol abuse — such as poverty, alienation, or lack of community — it focused on controlling behavior through external constraints. In doing so, it severed the connection between people and the natural rhythms of their lives, violating the principle of wuwei, or non-coercive action.

Socially constructed norms and values often carry the illusion of being objectively true when, in fact, they are subjective agreements shaped by culture, tradition, and power. The Daodejing implicitly challenges this illusion by revealing how these norms, such as what counts as good, beautiful, just, or proper, are not grounded in the Dao but in human convention. Once internalized, these constructs are mistaken for reality itself. People come to believe that there is a single, correct way to live, act, or appear, and they measure themselves and others against these standards. This can lead to rigid expectations, shame, exclusion, and constant pressure to perform according to external ideals, often at the expense of one's natural inclinations and well-being.

What makes these constructs especially problematic is that they become invisible — they shape perception and behavior without being recognized as arbitrary. For example, standards of beauty or success may feel universal, but they are highly contingent on time, place, and social context. The Daodejing warns against mistaking the label for the thing, the name for reality. The Daoist response is not to deny the existence of values altogether but to remain aware of their constructed nature — to hold them lightly and resist being ruled by them. By doing so, one can return to a more grounded, flexible, and attuned way of living — one that flows from the Dao rather than from the dictates of society.

Line (5) states the ideal that high De does not act on social constructs and is free from the assumptions that lead to believing the social constructions are objectively true. Whereas line (6) shows that low De is just the opposite:

5. High De does not act on social constructs
(wuwei) and is without assumptions (yiwei).
6. Low De acts on social constructs (wei) and has
assumptions (yiwei).

以為 (yǐwéi) the assumptions, is a way of describing the falling away from high De into increasingly artificial and self-conscious forms of moral behavior. In this context, yiwei signals the point at which De (as virtue) becomes something one tries to possess or display rather than something that arises effortlessly. It marks the beginning of moral posturing: acting not because it is in accord with the Dao but because one wants to appear good, follow rules, or uphold social norms. This distinction is at the heart of this chapter's layered critique of declining values, from effortless alignment with the Dao (high De) down through kindness, righteousness, and, finally, ritual.

Lines (7) - (10) examine how action and assumption play out in relation to three core Confucian values: kindness (仁 rén), righteousness (義 yì), and ritual (禮 lǐ) — the very pillars of moral life in the Confucian tradition.

7. High kindness (ren) acts on social constructs
(wei) and is without assumptions (yiwei).

In Confucian philosophy, 仁 (rén), often translated as "kindness," "benevolence," or "humaneness," is the core virtue that defines ideal moral character and right relationships. It represents a deep sense of empathy and care for others, rooted in the capacity to extend one's concern from the family outward to society at large. For Confucius, ren is not just a feeling but a cultivated disposition that enables a person to act with compassion, fairness, and respect in every situation. It reflects the ability to treat others as one would wish to be treated, and it is considered essential for creating a harmonious and orderly society. Importantly, ren is always relational; it arises through interpersonal engagement and is sustained by one's commitment to social roles and responsibilities.

The Confucian virtue of kindness sounds pretty good, so why would the Daodejing have a problem with valuing kindness? The Daoist issue with Confucian kindness is that it needed to be codified into a moral system that had to be taught and maintained in society. The codification of kindness, which is otherwise a natural and spontaneous human trait, is indicative of a broken social system that makes compassion and kindness a liability. When people are forced to compete with each other over socially constructed limited positions of rank and restricted resources, when people are taught socially constructed values that make some humans less important than others, when society rewards ruthlessness and success, then people need to be taught to be kind. Virtue kindness becomes a veneer over a rotten system that is slowly destroying natural kindness.

Line (7) sees the codification of kindness as the first consequence in the descent from De as the manifestation of Dao to De as a virtue. Because kindness can still be a natural response even within a destructive socially constructed context, high kindness is said to be without assumptions, as is high De.

> *8. High righteousness (yi) acts on social*
>   *constructs (wei) and has assumptions*
>   *(yiwei).*

In Confucian thought, 義 (yì), commonly translated as "righteousness" or "justice," refers to the moral disposition to do what is right, not out of personal gain or emotion, but because it aligns with ethical principles and one's duties within society. It emphasizes acting appropriately in context, especially when faced with difficult decisions where personal benefit must be set aside in favor of what is just and honorable. While ren (kindness) speaks to the inner motivation of empathy and care, yi speaks to the outer expression of moral integrity — the courage to uphold what is fair and proper even when it is difficult or unpopular. For Confucians, a virtuous person must embody both ren and yi: kindness guides the heart, while righteousness guides one's choices and behavior in the complex realities of social life.

From a Daoist perspective, 義 (yì) — righteousness or moral duty — is viewed with suspicion because it represents a stage in the decline from natural harmony into artificial moralism. This framing suggests that yi is not a sign of moral strength but a symptom of having drifted far from the effortless alignment with the Dao.

Daoists critique yi because it involves prescriptive judgment, imposing fixed standards of "right" and "wrong" that are often shaped by cultural norms or rigid traditions rather than rooted in the dynamic, living patterns of nature. Yi may compel people to act "correctly" by social standards. But, from the Daoist view, these actions are contrived, lacking the spontaneity and authenticity that arises from wuwei — action without forcing. Righteousness can quickly become performative and divisive, leading to moral superiority, coercion, and conflict. Rather than fostering true harmony, yi often enforces compliance with norms that may not reflect the deeper balance and interdependence of the world. High righteousness both acts on social constructs (wei) and has the assumption that the socially constructed values that define right and wrong are objectively true (yiwei).

9. *High ritual acts on social constructs (wei), but*
   when no one responds,
10. *Then arms are bared and [compliance] is*
    forced.

In Confucian philosophy, 禮 (lǐ), typically translated as "ritual" or "propriety," plays a foundational role in cultivating virtue and maintaining social harmony. It encompasses not only formal ceremonies and ancestral rites but also everyday behaviors — manners, etiquette, and proper conduct in various roles and relationships. For Confucius, li serves as a framework that shapes moral character through repeated practice. By performing rituals with sincerity and respect, individuals learn to embody values such as humility, loyalty, and reverence for others. Li thus functions as both a personal discipline and a social glue, reinforcing hierarchy, order, and continuity with the past. It is not viewed as empty formality but as a vital expression of inner virtue manifesting in outer action.

From a Daoist perspective, however, ritual is seen as a sign of decay — a compensatory structure that arises only after natural value has been lost. In this chapter, ritual is portrayed as the final rung in a descending chain; it is imposed to maintain social order. For Daoism, this signifies a significant disconnection from the Dao. Rituals are mechanical, hollow, and coercive, emphasizing appearances over authenticity and reinforcing artificial roles that distance people from their spontaneous, natural being. Rather than guiding people toward harmony, rituals can entrench conformity, suppress genuine emotion, and inhibit the fluid responsiveness that wuwei encourages.

Imagine a high official sees your young daughter, and her beauty enchants him. He takes her against her will, but because of his position, there is nothing anyone can do. He comes to you and presents the customary bride price for the defilement of your daughter. A price that is nothing to his wealth. Ritual is the socially constructed value that requires you to respectfully greet him and accept the payment with gratitude under the threat of punishment or death.

Line (10) expresses how far ritual has devolved in that it will resort to coercion and force to gain compliance. Daoism calls for a return to simplicity and directness, where people act not out of obligation or habit but from a deep and living resonance with the unfolding of the world.

This devolution of action is summarized in lines (11) - (14):

11. *When Dao is forgotten, De (as virtue) arrives.*
12. *When De (as virtue) is forgotten, kindness arrives.*
13. *When kindness is forgotten, righteousness arrives.*
14. *When righteousness is forgotten, ritual arrives.*

Lines (15) - (18)

The chapter then illustrates social problems that arise once devolved into ritual, beginning with the self:

15. *The ritualized self,*

The concept of "the ritualized self" describes a person who has surrendered their natural responsiveness to a life governed by external expectations, norms, and roles. This is the self shaped not from within but molded to conform to inherited scripts of virtue, propriety, success, or respectability, as prescribed by society. In this state, spontaneity is sacrificed for performance. One no longer asks, "What is called for in this moment?" but rather, "What am I supposed to do here?" This abdication of inner responsiveness is at the heart of the Daoist critique of 禮 (lǐ, ritual). When the natural way of De is lost, people turn to ritual as a substitute, mistaking outward correctness for authentic living.

In such a life, others are no longer encountered as living, dynamic beings but are instead filtered through the lens of expectation and utility. Relationships become transactional; people are seen not for who they are but for how they fulfill roles — as clients, competitors, partners, or obstacles. This mode of perception reduces the richness of human interaction to a series of strategic moves within a social framework. Compassion, curiosity, and genuine connection give way to manipulation, efficiency, and instrumental thinking. From the Daoist perspective, this is a metaphysical error. It reflects a failure to see the world as an unfolding whole, where each being is interrelated and continually transforming. The ritualized self, locked into a fixed role, cannot adapt to the flow of the Dao. It cuts itself off from the very source of vitality and wisdom that could guide it through a more responsive, alive way of being. Line (16) describes the ritualized self:

16. Is thin on loyalty and truth; confusion leads.

The ritualized self and the society that upholds it trade authenticity for appearances, ultimately sacrificing loyalty and truth in favor of conformity and stability. When individuals suppress their natural responsiveness in order to meet social expectations, their actions are no longer rooted in sincerity or insight but in obligation and performance. Loyalty, in its truest form, arises from deep relational awareness and mutual recognition — from seeing and being seen. However, within a ritualized framework, loyalty becomes a role to be enacted — a posture of allegiance to structure rather than to persons or principles. Truth, too, becomes compromised as individuals say and do what is expected rather than what is true to their understanding or experience.

This leads inevitably to confusion and alienation. People follow social scripts while feeling disconnected from their own motivations and from the genuine needs of those around them. Dialogue gives way to rehearsed interactions, and decisions are made not on the basis of insight or trust but on reputation, obligation, or hierarchy. In this climate, deception becomes normalized — not necessarily maliciously, but structurally. The truth of things is obscured by layers of ritual and expectation, leaving everyone to wonder what others really mean, feel, or intend. The Daodejing warns that when society loses the Dao and replaces it with constructs like virtue, righteousness, and ritual, it does not gain clarity but falls into contrivance and confusion.

The codification of socially constructed values is for the purpose of control. If a ruler is seeking their agenda rather than the good of the people, they need a mechanism for keeping people in line and respecting the chain of command. Additionally, they need a means to predict the future.

17. One foreknows

From a Daoist perspective, foreknowledge 前識 (qián

shí) represents a kind of intellectual preoccupation — an overreliance on planning, prediction, or calculated knowledge — that marks a subtle but dangerous departure from the Dao. It is not that knowledge itself is rejected, but that when knowledge becomes detached from direct experience and harmony with the present moment, it becomes disconnected from the Dao. Foreknowledge, in this sense, is artificial. It seeks to impose structure and control, anticipating outcomes rather than responding spontaneously to what arises. Line (18) continues by claiming that foreknowledge is thought to be an outcome from understanding the Dao, but in fact those who try to use foreknowledge are delusional.

18. [This is perceived as] the flowering of the
Dao, but it is the beginning of delusion.

The Daodejing critiques foreknowledge as the ornamental or superficial "flowering" of the Dao — something that looks impressive but lacks the depth and rootedness of the proper understanding of the Dao. Just as a flower is temporary and delicate, so too is foreknowledge: it can dazzle, but it quickly leads to 愚 (yú), meaning "folly" or "delusion." This folly arises when we mistake cleverness for wisdom and planning for clarity. In contrast, Daoist wisdom favors simplicity, receptivity, and direct perception. It values moving with the flow of things rather than trying to outthink or manipulate them.

The process of foreknowledge is fundamentally flawed because it depends on the illusion of complete, or at least, sufficient understanding — an illusion that the Daodejing challenges at its core. Human knowledge is always partial and selective. We can never grasp the full complexity of the world, let alone predict its unfolding with certainty. When we rely on foreknowledge to shape our actions, we place our trust in mental models and projections that are inevitably incomplete. Even a small gap in understanding — a detail overlooked, a variable unaccounted for — can lead to massive consequences, throwing off our predictions and undermining our plans.

This is especially true in dynamic, interconnected systems, where outcomes are shaped by countless subtle interactions. A decision made with apparent confidence may fail because it did not account for a cascading effect or an unseen influence. From a Daoist standpoint, this is not just a technical failure but a category error: it assumes that the world can be mastered through intellectual effort rather than engaged through presence and responsiveness. The delusion (愚) that arises from foreknowledge is not just about being wrong — it's about the hubris of thinking one can be certain in a world that is fluid, ambiguous, and perpetually in flux. Instead of clinging to foreknowledge, the Daodejing encourages a way of being that trusts the unfolding of things and responds with humility, adaptability, and deep attentiveness to the present.

Foreknowledge is a central component of modern business strategy. From quarterly forecasts and market analyses to five-year plans and algorithmic modeling, businesses rely heavily on the idea that with enough data and insight, the future can be anticipated and shaped. This approach mirrors the logic of foreknowledge critiqued in the Daodejing: it is based on the belief that accurate predictions enable effective control. But, like all expressions of foreknowledge, this method is limited by incomplete understanding, unpredictable variables, and the illusion of mastery in a world defined by complexity and change.

In practice, even the most sophisticated forecasting models can be undone by seemingly minor oversights — a shift in consumer behavior, a supply chain disruption, a new technology, or a political event. The 2008 financial crisis, the COVID-19 pandemic, and various technological disruptions (like AI and blockchain) all illustrate how systemic fragility and black swan events expose the weaknesses of predictive control. Businesses that rely too heavily on rigid planning can become brittle, unable to adapt quickly to unexpected events. Worse still, they may create harm by optimizing for short-term metrics or false certainties rather than cultivating sustainable relationships with people and ecosystems.

In light of this, the Daodejing offers a powerful alternative. Instead of trying to force outcomes through strategic foresight, business can be reimagined as a living, responsive process — one grounded in attentiveness, adaptability, and ethical responsiveness to change. Rather than relying on foreknowledge, we might emphasize co-creation, listening, iterative learning, and emergent design — principles aligned with wuwei, or non-forcing action. This does not mean abandoning planning altogether but holding plans lightly, staying open to feedback, and acting in ways that respect the complexity of interdependence. In this way, doing business becomes less about domination and control and more about cultivating resilience, trust, and harmony within a dynamic world. The problem of foreknowledge and the Daoist alternative are equally applicable to any kind of leadership, government, or other social institution.

Lines (19) - (22)

Having traced the decline from genuine "high" De to the increasingly artificial stages of kindness, righteousness, and ritual, this chapter now turns its focus to the implications of this descent for how one should live. The preceding lines have shown that when the Dao is lost, each successive substitute, no matter how well-intentioned, leads further from the source, ultimately creating division, pretense, and confusion. In light of this, the final lines offer an admonition to the reader, urging a way of being that resists this descent into contrivance. Rather than clinging to appearances or ideals, the great elder, a term for the ideal ruler here, stays rooted in what is thick and substantial, not thin and superficial, in what is real, not ornamental. This shift in emphasis moves the reader from critique to guidance: a call to reject the "flowers" of the Dao — its dazzling abstractions — and return to its deep, quiet roots.

19. Therefore, a great elder

20. Keeps to the thick and not with the thin,
21. Keeps to the fruit and not with the flower.
22. Thus, let go of that and hold on to this.

The core theme of Chapter 38 of the Daodejing is the decline from natural alignment with the Dao into increasingly artificial substitutes and the dangers of that descent. The chapter contrasts "high" De, which flows spontaneously and effortlessly from the Dao, with "low" De, a virtue that relies on intentional effort and moral willpower. It traces a progression: when true De is lost, people turn to kindness (仁 rén); when that is insufficient, they resort to righteousness (義 yì); when that fails, they fall back on ritual (禮 lǐ). This path marks a growing separation from the natural way — a shift from authentic responsiveness to contrived behavior governed by social expectations.

At its heart, the chapter is a critique of moralism and social virtue as replacements for the Dao. It suggests that the more society tries to enforce goodness through codified values and external actions, the farther it drifts from genuine harmony. The chapter warns that foreknowledge, cleverness, and overplanning may appear wise but are the beginning of folly. Thus, the great elder operates through wuwei (non-forcing), refusing to act from socially constructed ideals (為 wéi), and instead moves in alignment with the spontaneous unfolding of the Dao.

PART THREE
THE ART OF LIVING

As we now turn toward the Art of Living, I want to be clear about the spirit in which I offer what follows. This is not a set of instructions, nor a claim to mastery. I'm not here to prescribe what anyone should do. Instead, I'm sharing what I've done — and just as importantly, what I continue to do, and what I continue to struggle with. These reflections are drawn from my own attempts to live in alignment with the insights of the Daodejing, not as an authority but as a fellow traveler. This is a progress report, not a conclusion, the action component of the Way of Kinship.

The path shaped by the Way of Kinship is not something one completes, and it does not offer final answers. It offers a way of seeing, a way of being — a direction rather than a destination, a method rather than a conclusion. The insights I'll describe in the pages that follow are neither exhaustive nor universal. They emerge from my effort to live with greater clarity, responsiveness, and connection to the living world. I invite you to engage with them not as a system to adopt wholesale, but as seeds to plant, observe, and adapt to the conditions of your own life.

CHAPTER 8
WHAT AM I?

Asking the question, "What am I?" may seem strange at first, even less personal than the more familiar "Who am I?" But that's precisely the point. Asking "Who am I?" often leads us into the stories we tell about ourselves — names, roles, identities, reputations. These are shaped by culture, memory, and the expectations of others. They are helpful, but they don't reach the core. "What am I?" invites a different kind of reflection. It asks us to look beyond our personal narrative and consider our fundamental nature. What kind of thing is this that sees, feels, thinks, and moves? What is this process of being alive? Instead of reinforcing identity, the question gently dissolves it, revealing not a fixed self but a dynamic flow of experiences, perceptions, and relationships. In my own journey, it is this question — not who, but what — that has offered the clearest path forward.

When we understand what something is, we begin to

see more clearly how it functions and why it behaves the way it does. This is true of a machine, a tree, or a storm — and it's just as true of ourselves. If we think of ourselves merely as individuals with fixed identities and goals, we're likely to interpret our actions as products of will or choice alone. But if we come to see ourselves as living processes — shaped by biology, culture, memory, emotion, and the wider environment — then our behavior begins to make more sense. Patterns emerge. Habits become traceable. Emotions gain context. Struggles can be approached with more compassion and less judgment.

By asking, "What am I?" we create space to observe the structure and flow of our existence. And in doing so, we open ourselves to the possibility of change. When we understand how something works — including ourselves — we gain the ability to work with it rather than against it. This is not about control but about cooperation with our own nature. Understanding what we are becomes the foundation for living with greater clarity, resilience, and grace.

This line of inquiry is only possible because I am conscious. However, my consciousness is not omnipresent; it is situated in time and space and has a particular perspective. This leads to the first main point regarding what I am: I am embodied.

EMBODIED

The idea of being embodied challenges a long-standing cultural assumption: that we are something separate from our bodies, minds, or souls "inhabiting" a physical form. But from a modern scientific and cognitive perspective, this dualism doesn't hold up. We do not have a body as though it were an object we carry around. Instead, we are our bodies — living, sensing, responsive beings shaped by biology, movement, and experience. Every thought, feeling, and perception arises from processes in the brain and nervous system, which are, in turn, deeply interwoven with the body as a whole. Your heartbeat, your gut, your posture, your breath — all of these shape what you think and how you feel. To be a person is to be a body-in-environment, not a mind inside a shell.

Similarly, the phrase "I have thoughts" suggests that thoughts are possessions — things we control, own, or produce at will. But modern neuroscience paints a different picture. Thoughts arise from unconscious neural activity that becomes available to awareness after the fact. You don't "create" your thoughts so much as experience them. They are part of you, not separate tools or objects. More accurately, you are the process through which thoughts emerge and evolve. Cognitive science shows that attention, memory, language, and emotion are all deeply embodied — tied to movement, physical sensation, and past interaction with the world. So, to say "I am my thoughts" is to acknowledge that they are not something external or optional; they are part of the organism's total engagement with its world.

Mindfulness and secular Buddhism wisely remind us that we are not our thoughts — that is, we don't have to believe everything that arises in the mind, especially when those thoughts are harmful, repetitive, or distorted. This is a practical and compassionate teaching designed to help us distance ourselves from self-critical or anxious narratives. But what we're exploring here is something different: the ontological relationship between thought and self, not the psychological utility of stepping back from harmful thought patterns.

From a cognitive science perspective, consciousness is inseparable from thought. We cannot be conscious without some form of mental content — whether it's words, images, sensations, or emotional tones. Thought is not something that happens to consciousness; it is what consciousness is. Even when we feel like we're in a state of stillness or presence, subtle forms of conceptual processing or bodily awareness are unfolding. The brain is constantly generating patterns of activity, and what we call "a thought" is simply the segment of that process that becomes available to awareness.

That said, not all thoughts are created equal. Many of them emerge from unconscious, automatic processes — emotional residues, memory fragments, or conditioned responses. Some of these may be misaligned with our values, our current circumstances, or even reality. The key is not to deny that these thoughts are part of us but to recognize that we are not obligated to act on them. Just as our bodies produce sensations we don't always need to respond to (like a twinge or itch), our minds produce thoughts that may simply be noise — artifacts of stress, trauma, or old conditioning.

So yes, we are our thoughts in the sense that thought is a

natural function of being a conscious, embodied human. But we are also more than any single thought, and we can develop the awareness to observe our mental patterns with discernment.

Recognizing yourself as an embodied process — not a mind directing a machine, but a body-mind system inseparably unified — can be both unsettling and liberating. It reframes agency not as pure control but as participation. Your choices, habits, and experiences are not things you apply to your body and mind — they are your body and mind in motion. In this view, self-understanding becomes a matter of listening to and learning from your embodied experience rather than trying to dominate or escape it.

The Daodejing, while composed in ancient poetic language, resonates deeply with the idea of embodiedness, even though it doesn't frame it in the same terms as modern science. Several key themes suggest an understanding of the human being not as a disembodied mind or moral agent but as an integrated, responsive part of the natural world — a being shaped by breath, sensation, and participation in patterns far larger than the individual self. This leads to the second main point regarding what I am: I am embedded. In the Daodejing, the larger context in which we are embedded is the concept of oneness.

EMBEDDED

From the perspective of oneness, the embodied understanding of what I am becomes even more profound. If all things arise from the Dao and return to it, then there is no absolute boundary separating the self from the world. The body is not an object "in" nature; it is nature, no less than a river, a tree, or a cloud. To be embodied is not simply to inhabit a physical form — it is to be a living node in the vast network of interbeing. In this place, the Dao expresses itself moment by moment.

This understanding transforms our perspective on ourselves. If there is no separation, then the body is not just ours; it is the world folded into the shape of a human. It breathes the air, drinks the water, feeds on plants and animals, senses temperature and pressure, and responds to the gravitational pull of the Earth. It is permeable and co-created. Even our nervous systems — the roots of our sensations and thoughts — are shaped by our interactions with caregivers, communities, and environments. From the perspective of oneness, the body is not an edge but a meeting point: the place where sky, soil, and society converge into this ever-changing phenomenon we call "me."

This vision also reframes the relationship between mind and body. Thought does not hover above or beyond the world — it arises within the world as part of it. It is not an escape from embodiment but an expression of it. From this view, to live well is to live in rhythm with the whole. Embodiment is not a limitation but a gift: the very way we are able to relate, respond, and realize the unity of all things in a tangible, moment-to-moment way. Oneness is not something to believe in — it is something we inhabit with every breath, step, and heartbeat.

. . .

These concepts of embodied and embeddedness brought me two important insights. First, I am not the center of all things. Not that I was completely self-centered before, but I was moved to a deeper appreciation of my de-centeredness.

We all begin life from a naturally self-centered perspective — not out of arrogance or selfishness, but because of how consciousness first unfolds. From the moment we are born, everything we experience is filtered through our senses, our own body, and our mind. Hunger, comfort, fear, and attention all arise and are resolved from our point of view. This early self-centeredness is not a flaw; it is simply the starting point of awareness. As developing humans, we do not yet have the cognitive or emotional capacity to see beyond ourselves. The world seems to revolve around us because, in a very real sense, it does — subjectively.

But as we grow and interact with others, a crucial shift begins. We learn that other people have inner lives just as real as our own. We discover empathy, we experience loss, we negotiate fairness. Slowly, we come to realize that it's not all about me. This is the foundation of emotional maturity — the understanding that our wants, needs, and views exist within a web of relationships, not apart from them. We begin to de-center ourselves, not by erasing our identity, but by recognizing that our perspective is one among many and that the world is more complex than our immediate concerns.

The perspective of oneness deepens and completes this process of de-centering. It reveals that the self is not just one among many but a pattern within a larger whole — a wave in the ocean, not apart from it. Rather than clinging to a fixed identity, we begin to see ourselves as relational processes shaped by everything around us. Breath, thought, action, and even personality are not purely "ours" but arise through interaction with the environment, culture, language, and history. Oneness doesn't mean losing the self but understanding it more clearly: not as a separate entity, but as a node of consciousness through which the whole expresses itself.

In this light, maturity is not just about becoming less self-centered — it's about seeing the self more truthfully as one expression of a deeply interconnected and ever-changing reality. This de-centering does not diminish us. On the contrary, it grounds us in something far more vast, compassionate, and intelligent than the self alone could ever be.

When we begin to see ourselves as inseparable from the whole, something remarkable shifts: our identity, meaning, and sense of purpose are no longer confined to personal ambition or individual achievement. Instead, they arise from our place within the larger web of life. Who we are is not an isolated "self" trying to forge significance in a meaningless universe but a participant in a vast, dynamic system of relationships — biological, ecological, social, and cosmic. Our very being is sustained by breath from the atmosphere, food from the earth, and ideas passed down through culture. We are not self-made; we are world-made.

In this view, identity becomes a relational concept. I am a husband, a father, a son, a friend, a teacher, a listener, and a caretaker — not in a list of roles, but in the sense that my existence emerges through these relationships. I only come into focus when seen in connection with others. This doesn't negate individuality; it grounds it. My uniqueness is not lost in the whole — it is shaped by it, just as a single thread in a tapestry is defined by its connections to others.

Meaning, too, arises from participation, not possession. It's not something we extract from life but something we contribute to and discover within the ongoing flow of experience. We find meaning in moments of connection, in acts of service, in being part of something that extends beyond us. Purpose, then, is not a fixed destination but a quality of engagement — living in a way that affirms and supports the whole, even as we shape our small corner of it.

This shift doesn't erase suffering or struggle, but it reframes them. Instead of asking, "What does this mean for me?" we begin to ask, "What is my part in this larger unfolding?" In doing so, we align our lives with something more profound than the self, more enduring than success, and more generous than self-concern. Our identity, our meaning, our purpose — these are not private possessions but shared expressions of the greater whole we are always a part of.

One of the most powerful insights that comes from seeing ourselves as embedded within the fabric of life is the realization that no action happens in isolation. Every move we make is not simply our own — it is shaped by, and shapes, the patterns that surround us. This is what it means to say that all actions are co-actions. In other words, everything we do is a response to conditions we did not create alone, and everything we initiate ripples outward, influencing the conditions others encounter. Our lives are entangled — not metaphorically, but literally — in a web of relationships and causes.

The Dao, or the pattern of life, is not something outside of us, guiding us from afar. It is the ongoing flow of interactions — of nature, body, society, and mind — in which we are always participating. Our embeddedness in this flow means that outcomes are not the result of isolated will but of the interplay between our actions and the system of which we are a part. When we speak, we're not just choosing words; we're drawing on a shared language shaped by culture. When we build something, we're not just acting on materials; we're working within the constraints and affordances of the physical world, tools, time, and the actions of others.

Seeing all action as co-action dissolves the illusion of autonomy. Our choices matter precisely because they are part of something larger. We are never acting alone, and we never could. Even solitary acts, like thinking or breathing, are made possible by an ecosystem of prior events and ongoing support — air to breathe, thoughts passed down, and the conditions that gave rise to our existence.

Understanding this helps us become more skillful and compassionate. It encourages humility because we recognize that we are not the sole authors of our successes or failures. It promotes responsibility because our actions inevitably affect the system in which we live. It encourages curiosity because we begin to see that changing our lives and our world depends not on control but on learning how to better cooperate with the living patterns around us. To live well is to participate well — to act in ways that harmonize with the whole.

Frequently, discussions of co-action — the idea that all actions arise within a network of influences — lead naturally to questions about free will. This is especially true when people encounter the concept of determinism, the view that everything unfolds in accordance with prior conditions and the laws of nature. In the natural sciences, determinism is not a metaphysical claim but a foundational assumption: every event, from the movement of galaxies to the firing of neurons, results from a combination of the prior state of the system and the laws of physics — or in Daoist terms, the patterns (Dao) of everything.

The concern, then, is apparent: If everything is determined, how can I be free? If my thoughts, decisions, and actions are the inevitable outcome of causes that stretch back to before I was born, is there any room left for choice, agency, and responsibility?

The first challenge in answering this question is defining what "free" could actually mean in this context. If it means uncaused or outside of all influence, then the concept becomes incoherent. A genuinely free act, by that definition, would be random, disconnected from your personality, your goals, your past — more like the flip of a coin than a conscious decision. But that's not the kind of freedom we really want. We don't want our choices to be random — we want them to be ours. We desire to act in ways that reflect our character, embody our experiences, and respond skillfully to the world.

And here's the insight: those things — our history, our relationships, our accumulated understanding — are part of the prior state that shapes what happens next. They don't eliminate us; they constitute us. When we understand ourselves as learning beings embedded in a patterned universe, we stop chasing the illusion of metaphysical freedom and instead cultivate the kind of life that can act well within the patterns.

In the end, what we want is not to be "free" in some abstract, absolute sense but to be responsive, aware, and capable of growth. We want our actions to reflect who we are becoming through the ongoing process of living. That is not "free will" as usually conceived — it is something more grounded and more real. What we want is to be learning beings, not beings with "free will," whatever that could mean.

CHAPTER 9

RESPONSIBILITY AND COMPASSION

My reflections on what I am — fundamentally embodied and embedded — have restructured two primary lenses through which I see the world: responsibility and compassion.

The ancient philosophical concept of oneness and co-action helped me to grasp the modern scientific understanding of determinism. In determinism, what happens next is determined by the prior state of the system plus the laws of physics.

Picture a game of billiards. You strike the cue ball with your stick at a certain angle and speed. It rolls forward, hits another ball, and sends it ricocheting toward the corner pocket. Each movement — the roll, the collision, the new trajectory — is determined by the prior conditions: the speed and angle of the strike, the position of the balls, the texture of the table, and even the humidity in the room. If all the conditions were exactly the same, the result would be identical every time.

This is determinism in a straightforward, physical form: the present state and the governing laws of motion determine the next state. There's no mystery to it and no room for spontaneity outside of cause and effect.

Now, extend this image to yourself. You are vastly more complex than a billiard ball, but in principle, your brain, body, and environment are also governed by patterns — biological, psychological, social, and physical. Your actions are the result of billions of interrelated causes: genetics, neural activity, past experiences, relationships, and cultural influences. Like the cue ball, you're not acting in a vacuum. This is the interconnectedness and co-action of oneness.

But unlike a billiard ball, you are aware. You can observe patterns, learn from experience, and shift your behavior over time. That awareness doesn't exempt you from determinism — it's part of the causal chain. It means that your capacity to reflect, pause, and choose differently next time is itself a determining factor in what happens next and is, in fact, what determined you to make that choice.

Determinism raises serious and often uncomfortable questions about responsibility. If our decisions are the result of genetics, upbringing, environment, and past experiences — all factors we did not ultimately choose — then on what grounds can we say someone is genuinely responsible for what they do? If a person's actions were inevitable given their prior conditions, is it fair to praise or blame them? This challenges deeply held intuitions about moral accountability, justice, and even personal growth, calling into question the very framework by which we evaluate our behavior and that of others.

In the traditional view of responsibility, an individual is considered a free agent — someone who has the inherent ability to choose between different courses of action, independent of external causes or prior conditions. From this perspective, to be responsible means to have the genuine freedom to act otherwise and to be the sole originator of one's decisions. Praise and blame, reward and punishment, are justified on the grounds that the person could have made a different choice but didn't. This view places the individual at the center of moral evaluation, assuming a kind of internal sovereignty where actions emerge not as inevitable outcomes of cause and effect but as expressions of a freely willing self.

Imagine a manager named Lisa who angrily berates an employee during a meeting for missing a deadline, humiliating them in front of the team. Later, she expresses regret for her behavior, but the damage to morale has already been done.

From the traditional perspective, Lisa is fully responsible for her outburst. She could have chosen to respond calmly or to address the issue in private, but she didn't. The assumption is that she had the internal freedom to select among different options and, therefore, deserves to be held accountable for her poor choice. Her regret is seen as an acknowledgment of having violated an ethical norm that she could have upheld. In this view, corrective actions — such as formal apologies, disciplinary consequences, or ethical training — are seen as appropriate because she should have known better and could have acted differently.

From the perspective of determinism, Lisa's outburst is not evaluated as a free choice made in a vacuum but as the outcome of a long chain of prior causes. Perhaps she was under extreme pressure from upper management, had unresolved emotional patterns from past experiences, or had learned through previous professional environments that aggression gets results. Her actions are still serious and impactful, but rather than assigning blame in a moralistic sense, the focus shifts to understanding the conditions that led to the behavior. The goal is not punishment but transformation — changing the conditions that lead to such actions in the future, both in her and in the workplace culture around her.

Does this mean that there is no room for responsibility in a deterministic world? No, but it does change. To understand what responsibility might look like within a deterministic world, let's first reflect on what we are trying to achieve with responsibility.

The goal of responsibility is to maintain trust, promote accountability, and foster the conditions that enable individuals and communities to function effectively together. Responsibility serves as a framework for ensuring that actions have consequences, to guide behavior in ways that sustain cooperation, repair harm, and prevent future damage. It encourages reflection, fosters mutual respect, and enables systems of justice and learning to operate. Ultimately, the aim is to align behavior with shared values and improve the conditions under which better actions can emerge.

The goal of responsibility can still be met within a deterministic world. While a person's actions are the result of a long chain of events and causes outside of the individual's control, they are still the locus where the behavior arises. I find the author Paul Breer's term in his book, *The Spontaneous Self,* helpful: positional responsibility. With the concept of positional responsibility, we can still find a person's behavior acceptable or not according to the social norms we are seeking to uphold, but what changes is how we aim to encourage or discourage certain behaviors.

One of the more helpful analogies I have come across in explaining how to address unacceptable behavior is to treat it like a public health issue. When my son was a boy, if he caught a cold, we would not let him go to school. This was not a punishment; he did not choose to get a cold, but we did want to protect the other students from getting sick. While at home, we did what we could to help him get better. If we take this example to the extreme and imagine a contagious illness that was incurable, he would never be allowed back in public. However, his treatment would still not be to punish him but to do what we could to help with his condition.

. . .

To further illustrate how these perspectives might play out in real life, imagine a man named Derek who is arrested for burglary. From the traditional view, Derek is blamed for making a morally bad choice — he broke the law. He must be punished to atone for his wrongdoing and deter others. But from the perspective of positional responsibility within a deterministic framework, we ask a different set of questions: What led to this behavior? Perhaps Derek grew up in poverty, experienced early trauma, had little access to education, and lived in a community with few economic opportunities. These aren't excuses — they're causes. Derek is still the person through whom the act occurred, and society still has a duty to respond. But the response shifts from punishment to protection and transformation. Like isolating someone with a contagious illness, Derek may need to be removed from society temporarily — not to inflict suffering, but to prevent further harm and give him the best possible conditions for healing and change. This may involve therapy, skill-building, support networks, and a structured environment designed for rehabilitation. In this model, justice isn't about blame — it's about careful stewardship of social health, recognizing that changing outcomes means addressing causes.

This perspective also opens our eyes to a crucial truth: when we view harmful behavior as the result of complex causes rather than isolated choices, we are naturally led to examine the social systems that contribute to those causes. Derek's burglary, for example, cannot be fully understood or addressed without looking at the conditions of his neighborhood, the education system he passed through, the job opportunities available to him, and the structural inequalities he may have faced. The traditional view of responsibility, by focusing blame squarely on the individual, often functions as a kind of moral scapegoating — it allows society to avoid confronting the deeper systemic problems that may be creating patterns of harm in the first place.

When we treat wrongdoing solely as a personal failure, we obscure the role of social conditions in shaping behavior. This keeps us from asking hard questions about poverty, racism, mental health access, or institutional neglect. Positional responsibility, on the other hand, requires us to ask: What kind of world are we collectively creating? It acknowledges that individuals are not islands but expressions of their environments. If we want fewer acts like Derek's, we must improve not just Derek's life but the conditions that shaped it. In this way, shifting from blame to understanding doesn't weaken our sense of responsibility — it deepens it, expanding it from individual punishment to collective care and reform.

Just as a deterministic view challenges the idea of personal blame, it also complicates the notion of personal credit. If we acknowledge that harmful behavior arises from a network of causes beyond our control, the same must be said of positive actions, talents, and accomplishments. The gifted musician, the brilliant coder, the charismatic leader — none of these individuals created themselves. Their capacities are the result of genetics, early life influences, access to opportunities, mentoring, cultural context, and countless other factors. While we can and should appreciate excellence, we must also recognize that no one earns their raw abilities or the circumstances that allowed those abilities to flourish.

This doesn't mean we stop celebrating success or honoring achievement — it means we shift the emphasis. Instead of viewing rewards as a form of moral entitlement or superiority, we see them as a way of encouraging behavior and nurturing values within a broader system. For example, rewarding a scientist for a breakthrough is not a claim that they "deserve" it in some absolute sense; it's a way of highlighting and supporting work that benefits society. But this view also cautions us against unchecked meritocracy — the belief that the successful deserve their advantages simply because they succeeded. If talent and success are co-produced by circumstance, then compassion, equity, and shared investment become more important than ever.

Understanding reward in this way leads to humility and gratitude. It reminds us that our successes are not entirely our own and that lifting others up is not charity but an expression of truth: we are all part of the same unfolding network. This mindset encourages us not only to utilize our abilities wisely but also to create the conditions that enable others to thrive. In this sense, recognizing the limits of individual credit becomes a foundation for solidarity rather than competition.

· · ·

When I first began to seriously consider the deterministic view — that my thoughts, reactions, and choices all emerge from a web of causes beyond my control — it was unsettling. I had spent most of my life believing that I should have known better, should have tried harder, should have been different. That kind of internal moralism is exhausting. But as I began to understand that who I am is the result of a vast interplay of biology, experience, environment, and culture, something unexpected happened: I started to soften. I realized that many of the things I'd long punished myself for — my procrastination, my moments of anger, even deep regrets — were not signs of personal failure but expressions of patterns I hadn't yet fully understood. This view didn't absolve me of responsibility, but it transformed it. I became more interested in understanding how I work, how I'm wired rather than blaming myself for how I've acted.

And once I found that compassion for myself, it became easier — almost inevitable — to extend that same compassion to others. When someone hurt me or acted out of line, my first reaction used to be judgment. But now, I pause and wonder: What must have shaped them to respond this way? That doesn't mean I accept all behavior or let go of boundaries — it means I no longer need to frame others as monsters or villains. Like me, they are systems unfolding according to patterns. Some patterns cause harm, and we may need to intervene or protect others, but the intention shifts from punishment to understanding. This shift has changed my relationships. It's reduced my resentment. It's made space for connection where there was only defense before. And perhaps most profoundly, it's taught me that compassion isn't weakness — it's clarity. It's seeing the whole story behind every action and choosing to respond with wisdom rather than reacting on assumptions.

Compassion is at the heart of the Way of Kinship because it arises naturally from seeing ourselves and others as interconnected parts of a single unfolding process. When we understand that every action — our own and others' — emerges from patterns shaped by countless causes, we begin to let go of harsh judgments and begin to open ourselves to empathy. Compassion becomes a rational response to the truth of interdependence. It allows us to care for ourselves without shame and extend care to others without superiority. In a world where we are all co-creators of experience, compassion is the thread that binds us, guiding us toward healing, understanding, and collective well-being.

CHAPTER 10

NATURALISM AND SPIRITUALITY

Philosophical naturalism is the view that everything arises from and operates according to the principles of the natural world. It rejects supernatural explanations and instead holds that the universe and everything in it — including human thought, emotion, and society — are part of the same continuous reality governed by patterns, processes, and causes. This perspective emphasizes observation, coherence with the world as it presents itself, and an openness to the limits and wonder of what nature reveals. It views human beings not as separate from the cosmos but as embedded within it, emerging from it, and returning to it.

The Daodejing presents a profoundly naturalistic worldview. The text never appeals to supernatural beings, divine commandments, or metaphysical dualisms. Instead, it encourages readers to observe the Dao — the underlying Way or pattern of all things — as it manifests in the natural world. The sage, or wise person, is one who aligns with these patterns, not by imposing their will on the world, but by adapting to its rhythms, attending to what is overlooked, and yielding where others push. Nature, in the Daodejing, is not merely a backdrop to human activity — it is the very source and standard of wisdom. Water flows, the seasons turn, life emerges and dissolves — and so too should our actions arise naturally, appropriately, and without force.

This naturalism challenges anthropocentric values. The Daodejing subtly critiques human arrogance — the belief that with enough rules, rituals, and control, we can master the world. Instead, it invites a posture of humility, of learning from how nature works rather than trying to dominate it. It points us toward simplicity, quietude, flexibility, and attentiveness as guiding virtues — because these are the qualities that harmonize with the Dao, the ever-unfolding process of the world. In this way, the Daodejing presents a deeply rooted philosophical naturalism, a call to live well by living in harmony with the world rather than above or outside of it.

Earlier, I shared that I was once a Christian pastor. While I don't hold any hostility toward Christianity, my deepening commitment to a naturalistic worldview eventually made it impossible for me to remain within the Christian tradition. The transition wasn't easy — neither for me nor for those close to me. One of the most challenging questions I faced was what to do with my spiritual life. If I no longer believed in a supernatural framework, did that mean I had to abandon spirituality altogether? Or could there be a form of spirituality grounded in nature, rooted in experience, and consistent with a naturalist view of the world?

From a cognitive and psychological perspective, the human need for a spiritual dimension is not necessarily about gods, dogmas, or the supernatural. It is about meaning, connection, transcendence, and orientation. Neuroscience and psychology have demonstrated that our brains are wired for narrative, pattern recognition, and a sense of belonging to something greater than the isolated self. Practices often labeled "spiritual" — such as mindfulness, awe, ritual, and contemplation — activate brain regions associated with well-being, empathy, and integration. We crave coherence between our inner experience and the outer world, and we seek frameworks that help us make sense of our place in the vastness of existence. A naturalist spirituality doesn't suppress these needs; it honors them by redirecting them toward the real, the relational, and the deeply interconnected fabric of life.

Many people assume that the word spirit or the idea of spirituality automatically points to a supernatural worldview — something beyond nature, reason, or what can be known through science. In many religious traditions, spirit is often associated with disembodied forces, divine beings, or immortal souls. But this association is not inevitable. In fact, the root meaning of the word spirit tells a different story.

The word spirit comes from the Latin spīritus, meaning "breath," which itself comes from spirare, "to breathe." This connection to breath is profound. Breath is the invisible but vital process that animates life. We can't see it, but we can feel it. It sustains us, connects us to the living world, and reminds us of our embodied vulnerability. So when we speak of spirit in this original sense, we are not referring to something supernatural — we're referring to what makes life possible: the animating, flowing, vital processes that sustain our being. From this perspective, spirituality can be understood as the dimension of life concerned with nurturing that vitality — practices, reflections, and ways of living that promote well-being, clarity, connection, and meaning.

A naturalist spirituality, then, honors the breath-like essence of spirit without invoking the supernatural. It recognizes that awe, reverence, and deep interconnectedness are not irrational fantasies but rather core aspects of the human experience. It values silence, reflection, compassion, and presence — not because they please a deity but because they enrich the life of the individual and the health of the whole. Spirituality, understood this way, becomes a commitment to living in alignment with what is most real, most sustaining, and most life-affirming.

For me, spiritual practice has become less about finding answers and more about paying attention — a deep, steady kind of awareness that listens rather than declares. I no longer seek certainty or divine assurance; instead, I turn toward mystery. I spend time outdoors not to escape the world but to meet it. When I sit quietly and watch the way a tree moves in the wind or listen to bird song, I'm reminded of how much exists beyond my control or comprehension — and how beautiful that is. The natural world, when I let it in, softens my insistence on being the center of everything. I begin to feel more like a participant than a spectator, more like a thread in the tapestry than its designer.

That shift has altered how I perceive consciousness itself, a profound mystery in its own right. What continues to astonish me is that I am aware at all. That there is an inner light — this quiet knowing — that watches the world unfold through my senses and reflects on it. I didn't create this capacity. I didn't earn it. And yet it is here, moment after moment, allowing me to see, to feel, to wonder. I can't explain why awareness arises in this body; at this moment, I sit with the mystery. The fact of awareness is, in itself, enough to humble me and fill me with awe. It reminds me that being alive is not a problem to solve but a marvel to behold.

But the most transformative practice for me has been learning to honor the fleeting nature of the present moment. Everything I value — my breath, a kind word, a shaft of sunlight — arrives and then dissolves. Nothing stays, and yet everything matters. That impermanence used to frighten me. Now, it's what opens my heart. Knowing that no moment will last has made me more patient, more grateful, and more aware of the present. Spirituality, for me, is simply showing up fully, again and again, for the wonder of this moment — and letting that wonder shape how I live.

The Way of Kinship offers a form of spirituality grounded not in the supernatural but in the awe-inspiring reality of nature, relationships, and lived experience. For those of us who lean toward a naturalistic worldview — who trust in science, observe the patterns of the cosmos, and find meaning in this life rather than another — it provides a path of reverence without requiring belief in gods or metaphysical realms. It invites us to see ourselves as deeply embedded in the web of life, to recognize the beauty and fragility of the present moment, and to respond with compassion, humility, and care. This is a spirituality of belonging, not belief — a way of living that honors the mystery and interconnectedness of existence without stepping outside the natural world to do so.

CHAPTER II
HARMONY (和)

U p to this point, we have explored how perception shapes experience and how a shift in worldview toward interconnectedness, absence and presence, co-arising, and process can transform our actions in the world. These shifts begin on the inside, reorienting how we see ourselves and our place within the larger unfolding of life. Now we turn to harmony (和 hé), not just as an outcome of that transformation, but as a conscious strategy for living. Harmony offers a way to navigate the complexities of life — personally, socially, and environmentally — by aligning our actions with the patterns of the world. It is an embodied expression of the insights we've gained, applied moment by moment in how we move through life.

Producing harmony is not a passive state we fall into — it is an ongoing practice that requires sensitivity and skill. At its core, harmony arises from our ability to observe the world carefully, to pay attention to what is unfolding, and to respond in ways that support balance rather than disruption. Observation allows us to see not just what is happening on the surface but to sense the deeper patterns at play. Attention roots us in the present, helping us notice when something is moving out of alignment — within ourselves, in a relationship, or in the natural world. Adaptability gives us the flexibility to shift course, yield when needed, or hold steady when that is what the moment calls for.

These are not rigid techniques but dynamic skills — more like playing music than following a formula. To create harmony is to tune in to the moment and adjust with care, just as a musician listens to others in an ensemble. It requires humility, presence, and trust in the patterns that connect all things. In this way, harmony (和) becomes more than an ideal; it becomes a practice of living well, moment by moment, in relationship with everything around us.

Observation

Observation is a foundational skill for anyone seeking to live in alignment with the Dao. It is more than simply seeing — it is a form of deep noticing, an attentive presence to what is happening within and around us. In a world that rewards speed, productivity, and reaction, observation invites us to slow down and perceive rather than assume. It means listening before speaking, watching the patterns unfold before acting, and tuning in to subtle shifts that might otherwise go unnoticed.

In this way, observation becomes a discipline of attunement. The skilled observer detects nuance: a shift in tone, a change in mood, a slight imbalance in a system before it becomes a rupture. This awareness opens the possibility for a timely and wise response. We do not impose change; we respond to what is already taking shape. And that requires the patience to see clearly and the humility to admit that we may not yet fully understand.

Observation also helps us transcend our habitual filters. Often, we don't see what is there — we see what we expect. However, the deeper practice of observation interrupts this automatic mode. It becomes a practice of inquiry: What is really happening here?

The Daodejing frequently encourages noticing what lies beneath appearances, in the background, or in what is absent or empty, and elevates these subtle elements as essential to understanding how the world works. These moments are direct invitations to deepen observation beyond the obvious. Recall Chapter 11, for example:

Thirty spokes together form a hub
Its emptiness (無 wú) is necessary
To have (有 yǒu) a useful cart.

Mold clay into a vessel
Its emptiness (無 wú) is necessary
To have (有 yǒu) a useful vessel.

Construct doors and windows into a room
Their emptiness (無 wú) is necessary
To have (有 yǒu) a useful room.

Therefore,
To have (有 yǒu) makes benefit
Emptiness (無 wú) makes useful.
(Chapter 11)

This passage is a classic Daoist teaching in the art of reversing our habitual focus. Most of the time, our attention is drawn to what is visible, tangible, and measurable — the spokes of the wheel, the clay of the pot, the walls of the house. We instinctively identify the "thing" with its physical substance, believing that its value lies entirely in what has been added, shaped, or built.

The Daodejing invites us to look deeper — or rather, to look through. The wheel turns not because of the spokes, but because of the empty space at its hub. A pot is useful not because of the clay itself, but because of the hollow it contains. A house shelters us not by its walls alone, but by the open space within.

In each case, the wú (non-being) is what makes the yǒu (being) truly functional. Without emptiness, the form has no purpose. This is not just a clever observation about carpentry or pottery — it is a shift in perception. It trains us to see what is usually overlooked: the absence, the openness, the hidden condition that makes use possible.

Applied more broadly, the teaching becomes a guide for

life. In relationships, it is often the listening (the space for another's voice) that makes connection possible. In leadership, it may be the restraint from over-controlling that allows a team to flourish. In art, it is the silence between notes that gives music its shape.

By attending to what is not there — to the background, the pause, the gap, the stillness — we begin to notice that usefulness often depends more on emptiness than on substance. This reorients us toward humility: the most powerful contributions in life may be the ones we cannot grasp, measure, or even name, yet without them, nothing works.

Another key passage on observation is found in Chapter 10:

Cleanse [your] dark mirror
Can [you do so] without flaws?

This phrase evokes the metaphor of the heart-mind (心 xīn) as a mirror — a surface that reflects the world as it is. A clear mirror is one that responds to what appears without clinging, distorting, or reacting to preconceptions. It doesn't hold onto past reflections nor anticipate future ones. It reflects accurately and impartially.

Another Daoist writing from the same period as the Daodejing is the Zhuangzi (Pronounced roughly: Jwahng-dzuh), which also explores this idea.

The Perfect Man uses his mind like a mirror —

going after nothing, welcoming nothing,
responding but not storing."
(Chapter 7, Watson)

While mirrors today are shiny and bright, ancient Chinese bronze mirrors were dark and polished, unlike the glass mirrors of today. They required constant maintenance and cleaning to maintain their reflective quality. But "dark" here is not just a description of the color; it is another use of the character 玄 (xuán) we saw in Chapter 1 of the Daodejing, where we read:

Call this unity darkness,
darkness within darkness,
the entrance to all mysteries.

The character 玄 (xuán) is often translated as "dark" or "mysterious," but in the Daodejing, its meaning runs far deeper. It points not merely to visual obscurity but to that which is beyond direct grasp — something subtle, profound, and hidden from ordinary perception. 玄 suggests the depths of reality, the unseen forces, and patterns from which all things emerge. It resonates with the Daoist emphasis on yin-like qualities: absence, receptivity, and stillness. In this sense, 玄 reflects the priority of the unseen — the space behind the form, the silence beneath the sound, the emptiness that gives rise to presence. It calls us to attend to the layers of reality that are not immediately visible or nameable but are essential to the unfolding of all things. In doing so, it invites a kind of perception that honors the primacy of what cannot be pinned down, not as a void, but as the fertile ground of transformation and unity. Achieving this level of vision requires clear reflection.

In ancient Chinese thought, water and mirrors symbolized stillness, clarity, and receptivity. A still pond or reflecting pool was a symbol of the unperturbed mind. This symbolism blends 心 (xīn, heart-mind) as both emotional and cognitive — the faculty that needs to be stilled and clarified for wisdom to arise.

The clear, dark mirror reflects whatever is before it without preference, without self. It doesn't resist or grasp. This is the model of the sage's awareness — pure, open, and always in the present. If spots appear — expectations, judgments, identities — they cloud the surface and distort the reflection. This image is an invitation: Can you cleanse your dark mirror? Can you see the world clearly without yourself always in the way?

Observation is a disciplined art of seeing, not just looking, but truly perceiving. It begins when we slow down enough to notice what is often overlooked: the background, the empty space, and the quiet shift before the change. This kind of seeing breaks through the automatic filters of habit and expectation. It is the foundation of wisdom and harmony because it aligns our awareness with what is actually unfolding, not what we wish or assume to be.

This level of observation is deeply tied to the Daoist understanding of the mysterious, or 玄 (xuán), the subtle and unfathomable aspects of the world. The sage, like a dark mirror or a still pool, reflects without interference, welcoming what is present without imposing form or judgment. Observation, then, is more than a mental act; it is a spiritual discipline that clears the surface of the self so that the Dao — the deep pattern of the world — can be seen and followed.

Attention

Attention is one of the most powerful practices available to us, and yet it often slips by unnoticed. In a world filled with distraction, divided focus, and constant stimulation, the act of paying attention — truly attending to what is here — becomes a radical, grounding force. Attention anchors us in the present moment. It pulls us out of the swirl of anticipation and memory and roots us in the reality of now, where life is actually happening.

To practice attention is to bring the fullness of our awareness to what we are doing, sensing, or witnessing — without rushing to judgment, without immediately narrating or categorizing. Whether it's the feel of our breath, the tone of a conversation, the warmth of sunlight, or the tension in our chest, attention invites us to inhabit the moment fully. In doing so, it transforms the ordinary into something intimate and alive.

This grounding quality of attention is participatory. Attention enables us to perceive the world as it is rather than as we assume or wish it to be. It fosters clarity, connection, and even compassion. When we attend deeply, we begin to notice patterns, needs, and possibilities that are otherwise missed. Attention becomes the gateway to responsiveness — the kind of responsiveness that flows in harmony with the world, not in conflict with it.

In this way, attention is not just a tool of mindfulness but a foundational act of presence. It is how we meet life — with eyes open, with heart attuned, and with a willingness to see what is actually there.

Here are some practical ways to develop attention and strengthen your capacity to be present in daily life. While not taken directly from the Daodejing, these practices align well with its spirit of observation, stillness, and attunement to the natural flow of things.

1. Single-Tasking

Choose one activity — eating, walking, or even washing the dishes — and give it your full attention. Put away distractions. Feel the texture of the food, notice the rhythm of your steps, and observe the temperature of the water. The goal is not to think about the task but to experience it directly.

This cultivates presence by anchoring awareness in the sensory moment rather than in abstraction or planning.

2. Breath Awareness

Set aside a few minutes each day to sit quietly and observe your breath. Don't try to change it; simply notice the inhale, the exhale, and the space between. When your mind wanders, gently return to the breath.

This is a simple but powerful tool to return to the present and train the mind to recognize when it has drifted.

3. Pause Before Responding

When you feel a strong impulse to speak, react, or decide — pause. Even a few seconds of silence creates space to observe your internal state and the external context. In that pause, ask: What's really happening here?

This helps shift from reactive to responsive behavior — a core element of conscious attention.

4. Journaling

Spend a few minutes each evening reflecting on where your attention was during the day. What moments were you honestly present for? When were you distracted? What did you notice that you might have missed before?

Journaling sharpens your observational mind and reveals patterns in how you relate to your experience.

5. Nature Immersion

Go outside without a goal. Sit in a park or stroll through a forest or garden. Use your senses: feel the air, listen to sounds, watch the way light moves through leaves. Let your surroundings guide your attention.

Nature's patterns — irregular, subtle, and emergent — are ideal for cultivating a patient and open kind of attention.

6. Body Scanning

Lie down or sit comfortably and bring attention systematically to different parts of your body. Notice sensations without judgment. This not only fosters presence but also reconnects you with your embodied experience — a crucial foundation for awareness.

7. Digital Boundaries

Try creating "attention sanctuaries" — periods where you silence devices and avoid media. Start with 30 minutes a day. These boundaries give your nervous system space to recalibrate and your attention time to strengthen.

Attention is like a muscle: it grows with intentional, consistent use. These practices aren't about perfection — they're about returning again and again to the present. Over time, you may find that the world seems richer, your relationships deeper, and your actions more aligned with what truly matters.

When we talk about attention — how to improve it, cultivate it, and maintain it — we often focus on psychological strategies or mindfulness practices. However, one vital element is frequently overlooked: nutrition. The brain is not an abstract processor floating outside biology;

it's a highly demanding organ that consumes a disproportionate amount of the body's energy. If we want to function at our best mentally, we need to give the brain the right fuel.

This is a large and evolving topic, and different people respond to other approaches. What I can offer here is not a prescription but a personal account of what has worked for me in boosting mental clarity, sustained attention, memory, and processing speed. You will need to conduct your own research and consult with a healthcare professional before starting new supplements or dietary protocols. Individual biochemistry varies, and what works well for one person may not be suitable for another.

1. Low-Carb, Ketogenic Diet

Adopting a low-carbohydrate, high-fat ketogenic diet has had the most noticeable and sustained effect on my ability to focus. By shifting my metabolism from glucose to ketones as a primary fuel source, I've experienced more stable energy throughout the day and significantly less mental fog. Ketones are a more efficient fuel for the brain in many ways, and they reduce the blood sugar crashes that often come with high-carb meals. This alone has made it much easier to engage in long periods of deep work and sustained attention. Please do your research and consult your medical provider before making radical changes in your diet.

· · ·

2. Creatine

Though primarily associated with athletic performance, creatine also plays a role in brain energy metabolism. In the body, creatine helps rapidly regenerate adenosine triphosphate (ATP) — the primary energy currency of cells. While muscles are the most obvious beneficiaries during short bursts of activity, the brain also relies heavily on ATP to fuel processes like neurotransmission and maintaining cellular health. By increasing the amount of phosphocreatine stored in the brain, supplementation provides a quick-access energy reserve that can sustain mental performance during prolonged or demanding tasks. Supplementing with creatine has given me a noticeable boost in mental stamina, especially when working through cognitively intense projects. There is growing scientific support for creatine's role in brain health, with studies exploring its potential benefits for memory, fatigue resistance, and even resilience under sleep deprivation.

3. Coffee

It's no surprise that caffeine supports alertness, but I've learned that its timing and form matter. Strong coffee in the morning sharpens my focus without disrupting my sleep, as long as I stop before 11 AM. Pairing caffeine with fat, such as butter and MCT oil (as in "bulletproof coffee"), seems to smooth the energy curve and reduce the jitters. For me, this combination increases alert calmness, a state ideal for attentive presence.

. . .

Attention is not just a mental phenomenon — it's embodied. It depends on physiology, energy balance, and chemistry. Our brains need proper fuel, and tweaking that fuel has been one of the most effective ways I've found to support the attentional practices I care about. Just as a high-performance machine needs clean inputs to run smoothly, so too does the mind.

In addition to nutrition, movement plays a vital role in sustaining and enhancing attention. Regular physical activity not only improves blood flow and energy metabolism in the brain but also sharpens mental focus and protects against cognitive decline over the long term.

While aerobic exercise like walking, jogging, or swimming provides broad benefits — including boosting mood, oxygenating the brain, and stimulating neurogenesis — coordinated, mindful movement practices offer even more. Activities like yoga, tai chi, and dance combine complex motor skills with rhythm, timing, breath, and attention. These practices train the brain and body together, building what neuroscientists refer to as sensorimotor integration. This integration supports better balance, focus, memory, and even emotional regulation.

For example, yoga engages strength, flexibility, breath awareness, and focus. Moving slowly and deliberately through postures while monitoring your breath demands sustained attention. Similarly, tai chi, with its continuous flowing movements, is like meditation in motion. It has been shown in clinical studies to improve executive function, attentional control, and working memory.

Dance adds the cognitive challenge of music, timing,

and improvisation, which further stimulates brain plasticity. Coordinated movement, especially when learned in community or group settings, also supports emotional health, social bonding, and resilience — all of which contribute to our capacity to stay present and attentive in daily life.

In my own experience, these practices don't just sharpen the mind — they help unify it with the body. Attention trained in movement carries over to stillness, helping me focus better when reading, writing, or engaging with others. Just as we nourish the brain with the proper fuel, we nourish attention with intentional movement. The body is not a distraction from awareness — it is a doorway into it.

Adaptability

In a world shaped by co-dependent origination, no person or event arises in isolation. Every agent — whether a person, system, or organism — is deeply embedded in a web of relationships, constraints, and possibilities. This means that every situation we encounter is a dynamic convergence of forces, histories, contexts, and perspectives. As such, an action that worked for a similar situation may not always be appropriate, as no two situations are ever precisely the same. Instead, each moment asks something different of us, and meeting it well requires the ability to perceive its distinct character and respond accordingly. This is the essence of adaptability.

Adaptability is the art of attunement — of being responsive without being reactive, of sensing not only what is happening but what the situation is becoming. Because all action is co-action, and all doing is inter-doing, our responses are never isolated efforts. They ripple through the web of relationships, producing new constellations of cause and effect. The more we learn to observe, pause, and sense the direction of flow rather than impose a fixed agenda, the more we can act skillfully within the whole.

This brings us to the goal of harmony (和 hé), a dynamic equilibrium among changing forces. To live harmoniously is to move with the currents of co-dependent origination, not against them. This requires humility, flexibility, and awareness — recognizing that what we do affects everything else and that wise action involves aligning ourselves with the broader patterns of life.

In this view, adaptability becomes a kind of ethical intelligence — the ability to find the most generative path through complexity. Harmony is not the absence of tension but the ability to navigate tension without collapse. When we cultivate adaptability, we are not merely surviving in a changing world; we are participating in the ongoing unfolding of reality with skill, grace, and compassion.

CULTIVATING INNER HARMONY

Harmony (和) is not merely a social or environmental principle. It is just as critical in the interior landscape of our own hearts and minds. In the Daoist worldview, there is no separation between the self and the world. How we perceive and respond to the world is shaped by the internal state of our 心 (xīn), the heart-mind. This term in Chinese thought encompasses both emotion and cognition, as well as feeling and understanding.

Emotional Regulation and the Mirror Pool of the Heart

In Daoism, xīn is often likened to a mirror pool. When the surface is calm and undisturbed, it reflects the world clearly and without distortion. But when stirred by emotional turmoil, it ripples and warps the image it receives.

This metaphor of the mirror pool is a powerful one. It teaches us that emotional regulation is not about suppressing or controlling emotions but about cultivating a state of inner calm and responsiveness. When the heart-mind is clear and undisturbed, it is capable of perceiving the interconnected reality of all things. When agitated, it imposes its own distortions, which in turn affect how we act and how the world responds to us. Emotional regulation, then, becomes essential for harmony at all levels.

Emotional Ripples and Distortion

Emotions such as anger, anxiety, jealousy, or resentment can be understood as winds that disturb the surface of the mirror pool. They do not arise independently. They are conditioned responses to situations shaped by our past experiences, expectations, and attachments. When we experience these emotions, we mistake their distorted reflections for the world itself. We act based on our misperceptions, and our actions generate further disruption.

For example, consider a moment of anger in response to a perceived insult. If the heart-mind is disturbed, it may magnify the insult, assuming intent or meaning that may not exist. In turn, we respond defensively or aggressively, escalating conflict. But if we can observe the emotion without being swept up in it, we may recognize the insult as a passing ripple, not a fixed reality. This recognition enables a more skillful and appropriate response.

Reframing Through Oneness

The Way of Kinship invites us to reframe our emotional experiences through the lens of oneness. From this perspective, nothing arises independently. Our feelings are not private, autonomous phenomena; they are products of our embeddedness in a network of relationships. We feel what we feel because of our history, our culture, our biology, and the circumstances of the present moment. Recognizing this interdependence reveals the possibility of reframing the situation.

Reframing does not mean denying our feelings; it means reevaluating them. It means seeing our emotions as part of a larger pattern. When we feel anxiety, for instance, we can pause and ask: What is this anxiety responding to? What expectation or narrative is shaping this response? Can I shift my perspective and see this moment differently? Often, a change in frame — seeing the event not as a threat but as a challenge, not as a judgment but as a misunderstanding — can soften the emotion and allow for greater clarity.

Reframing is supported by the Daoist concept of impermanence. No emotional state is fixed. All things arise and pass away. By observing the temporary nature of emotions, we can learn not to cling to them or fear them. We let them come, we let them go. This attitude of non-attachment is a form of gentle openness, a willingness to feel without being consumed by emotions.

Techniques for Emotional Regulation

While the Daodejing emphasizes natural responsiveness and alignment with the Dao, modern cognitive science offers complementary techniques that help stabilize and clarify the heart-mind. Many of these techniques align well with Daoist sensibilities.

1. Breath Awareness

Breath is the most immediate tool we have for calming the nervous system. Deep, slow breathing activates the parasympathetic nervous system, which helps bring us out of states of stress and reactivity. A simple practice: take five deep breaths, focusing on the sensation of air entering and leaving the body. Let your attention follow the breath without judgment. This alone can begin to still the surface of the mirror pool.

2. Labeling Emotions

Research in affective neuroscience shows that labeling an emotion can reduce its intensity. Simply saying to yourself, "This is anger," or "This is fear," creates a bit of distance between the emotion and your sense of identity.

3. Cognitive Reappraisal

Cognitive reappraisal is a modern version of reframing. When something triggers an emotional response, pause and reflect: Is there another way to view this? Could this be an opportunity? A misunderstanding? A moment to learn something new about myself? This practice fosters adaptability and reduces rigidity.

4. Grounding in the Body

Returning awareness to the body can help dissolve emotional storms. Emotions are not just mental; they are physiological. Feel your feet on the ground, your breath in your chest, the temperature of your skin. These sensations can help bring you back to the present moment and reduce the grip of emotional narratives.

· · ·

5. Cultivating Gratitude

The practice of gratitude can shift emotional tone and broaden perspective. By attending to what is going well, we expand our view and re-center ourselves in the unfolding harmony of life.

Everyday Examples of Harmonizing Within

Imagine waking up late and rushing to get ready. As you're hurrying, you spill your coffee. In a reactive state, you might slam the cup down, curse, and let the frustration ruin your mood. But with practiced observation, you might notice the tension rising and pause. You take a breath. You recognize the ripple and its source. You reframe the situation: it's a minor setback, not a catastrophe. The emotion passes, and you regain your center.

Or consider a tense conversation with a friend. Their words hit a nerve. The mirror pool begins to ripple. But rather than respond immediately, you take a moment. You ask, "Why did that bother me so much? What story am I telling myself about what they meant?" You realize you're responding not to what they said but to an old wound. You name the emotion. You breathe. You ask for clarification rather than attacking. The result is harmony, not rupture.

Yet emotional distortion does not arise only from raw feelings. The ripples on the mirror pool are further disturbed by the sediment of inherited biases and false social constructs. These are the stories we are told about who we are and how the world works: about gender, race, success, failure, virtue, and value. They influence our perception even before an emotional reaction arises. If the mirror pool has already been dyed by ideology, then even a still surface reflects a distorted world.

Take, for example, the notion of worthiness being tied to productivity. In many cultures, we are taught that rest equals laziness and that constant output is the measure of value. When we pause or feel tired, shame may arise — not because of the actual experience of rest, but because of the socially constructed story that has infiltrated the mirror pool. Without questioning these assumptions, we are not truly seeing — we are projecting.

Daoist practice invites us to clear the mirror not only of emotional agitation but of these more subtle and insidious distortions. This requires both observation and critical awareness. We begin to ask: Where did this belief come from? Who benefits from this value system? Is this interpretation helping or harming the harmony of my inner state?

Adopting the perspective of oneness helps loosen the grip of rigid social narratives. When we see ourselves not as isolated agents but as participants in a co-emergent process, we no longer need to uphold an identity shaped by unrealistic or harmful ideals. Instead, we can begin to honor the rhythms of our own body-mind, adaptively responding to life as it unfolds.

The Mirror as a Practice

. . .

Our inner state, our mirror pool, requires attention and care. The goal is not perfection but clarity. We will always experience emotion. The key is how we relate to those emotions — with curiosity, with space, with a sense of their arising as part of the dance of Dao.

Harmony is not a fixed state. It is a skillful, flexible balancing. It grows from observation, reframing, and adaptability. In this sense, emotional regulation is not just about feeling better; it is about seeing better. And through that seeing, acting in ways that contribute to the unfolding harmony of the world.

Next, we will examine how this inner harmony relates to the social and environmental aspects of harmony. But it all begins here, in the still waters of the heart-mind. Can you cleanse your dark mirror without flaw? Can you see clearly enough to move in alignment with the Dao? The practice begins with presence, attention, and a willingness to see what is there, not what we wish were there.

CULTIVATING SOCIAL HARMONY

Having explored the importance of cultivating harmony within, we now turn our attention to harmony in the social domain. Social harmony, like inner harmony, is not a fixed state but a dynamic process that requires continuous engagement. It involves attention, adaptability, and the recognition that human relationships are embedded in larger networks of mutual influence and interconnection. In a world marked by diversity of views, conflicting needs, and historical injustices, social harmony may seem like a lofty ideal. Yet the Daodejing offers a clear and practical orientation: harmony is not uniformity or suppression of difference, but the skilled and compassionate weaving of relationships in accordance with the patterns of life.

Harmony and conformity are often mistaken for one another, but they operate on fundamentally different principles. Conformity demands uniformity — a suppression of difference in favor of consistency, predictability, and control. It prioritizes agreement over authenticity and often pressures individuals to conform to a pre-established mold, regardless of personal traits or situational nuance. Harmony, by contrast, recognizes the value of difference and seeks to integrate it. In a harmonious system, diversity of roles, perspectives, and temperaments enriches the whole, just as distinct instruments contribute to the beauty of a musical ensemble. While conformity is threatened by deviation, harmony thrives on it. Harmony does not erase difference; it attunes it into a dynamic and responsive whole.

In cooking, if all the ingredients were the same — say, only flour — you would be limited in what you could create. Every dish would be bland and one-dimensional. But when you harmoniously combine varied ingredients, balancing flavors, textures, and aromas, you unlock the possibility of a far more delicious and nourishing meal.

The same is true in music. Conformity would be like having every instrument play the same note at the same time — technically unified, but dull and lifeless. Harmony allows for different notes, rhythms, and timbres to interact, creating chords, melodies, and counterpoints. The result is richer, more dynamic, and far more moving than any single, unvaried sound could ever be.

The Chinese character for harmony, 和 (hé), is composed of two parts: the character for grain and the character for mouth. Together, they suggest the image of sharing a meal or coming to an agreement at the table. This metaphor highlights the interpersonal nature of harmony — it is not something achieved in isolation but through dialogue, coordination, and mutual respect. When we reflect on social systems, whether families, communities, workplaces, or governments, the metaphor of a shared meal remains a valuable lens. What is being cultivated, distributed, or withheld? Who is being fed, and who is being silenced?

Observation in Social Contexts

Just as observation is vital to inner harmony, it is crucial in social settings. The ability to truly see another person, to notice their tone, body language, emotional state, and unspoken needs, lays the foundation for mutual understanding. Chapter 49 of the Daodejing states:

> *The sage has no set mind,*
> *He takes the mind of the people as his mind.*
> *(Chen)*

This does not mean the sage is passive or without values, but rather that they are deeply attentive and receptive to the experience of others. They do not impose their own agenda prematurely. In practical terms, this might look like listening deeply in a conversation before offering advice or pausing to understand someone's circumstances before making judgments.

The modern practice of active listening mirrors this Daoist insight. Active listening involves more than just hearing words; it is the art of suspending one's inner chatter and judgments to fully attend to the speaker. It requires humility and patience — virtues central to Daoist thought. The social harmony fostered by such listening is not simply peaceful interaction; it is a more accurate alignment with reality. We can better understand each other and thus respond to each other more effectively.

Timing is also important; consider Chapter 64:

> *A tree too big to embrace*
> *Is born from a slender shoot.*
> *A nine-story tower*
> *Rises from a pile of earth.*
> *A thousand-mile journey*
> *begins with a single step.*
> *(Addiss & Lombardo)*

These lines highlight the importance of responding appropriately at the earliest stages of interaction. If we wait until a conflict is full-blown, it is harder to restore harmony. But if we are attuned to subtle tensions, minor misunderstandings, or brewing resentment, we can adapt and redirect more easily.

Imagine two coworkers who have a minor disagreement over how to handle a project detail. At first, it's just a passing comment that feels slightly dismissive, but neither addresses it. If they ignore it, small slights and assumptions build until the tension becomes a full argument that damages their working relationship.

If, instead, one notices the early discomfort and says, "I think we might see this differently—can we talk it through?" the conversation stays manageable. Like tending a young sapling rather than trying to straighten a full-grown tree, addressing the issue early makes it far easier to restore harmony.

Adaptability in social relationships does not mean abandoning our principles. It means adjusting our approach, not our integrity. It is about choosing our response in a way that aligns with the flow of the situation and our deeper values.

In psychological terms, this adaptability aligns with emotional intelligence, which is the capacity to recognize emotions in ourselves and others and to respond skillfully. In team settings, for example, the emotionally intelligent person can sense when morale is low, when someone feels excluded, or when a decision is not sitting well with them. They don't need to assert control; they facilitate realignment. This is a modern echo of the Daoist sage, who governs not by force but by presence and perception.

Non-Contention and Non-Forcing

One of the most repeated principles in the Daodejing is that the sage does not contend. Chapter 8 compares the sage to water:

> *The highest adeptness is like water.*
> *Water's adeptness benefits the ten thousand*
> *things without contending.*

Non-contention does not mean withdrawal or avoidance. It is a refusal to engage in ego-driven struggle. In social terms, this could be like declining to escalate an argument, even when one feels insulted. It might look like offering a generous interpretation of someone's words rather than assuming ill intent. This approach fosters safety and reduces reactivity in groups.

There are many examples in daily life where non-contention can be a transformative force. In workplaces, for instance, turf wars and politics often arise from insecurity and a perceived scarcity of recognition or power. A Daoist approach would counsel us to step back from these battles, to let go of the need to be seen as right or superior, and to focus instead on the underlying purpose of the work. In family settings, where long-standing histories and emotional patterns run deep, non-contention can mean breaking the cycle of accusation and defensiveness and instead speaking from a place of vulnerability and care.

Compassion and Forgiveness

Social harmony cannot be sustained without compassion. This is not a sentimental or performative compassion but one rooted in the understanding of our shared embeddedness. When we realize that everyone is a product of countless conditions — genetic, cultural, and circumstantial — our perspective shifts. We move from blame to inquiry, from judgment to curiosity.

This understanding supports forgiveness. Forgiveness does not mean condoning harm or relinquishing accountability. It means recognizing that punitive attitudes often perpetuate cycles of harm. When we forgive, we break the cycle of resentment. A better word would be acceptance rather than forgiveness. We make space for restoration. The concept of positional responsibility discussed earlier applies here. We hold others responsible in the sense of needing to address the consequences of their actions, but we do so in a way that seeks healing, not punishment.

In this light, restorative justice models offer a modern approach aligned with the Daoist ideal. They focus not on retribution but on repair: what harm was done, how can it be made right, and how can the community be strengthened in the process? This is social harmony in action.

· · ·

Shared Goals, Not Uniformity

Social harmony is sometimes confused with consensus or sameness. But harmony, as in music, involves different tones working together. The Daodejing embraces paradox and difference. Chapter 42 observes:

> *The ten thousand beings carry yin on their backs*
> *and embrace yang in the front.*
> *Blending these two vital breaths (qi) to attain*
> *harmony (he).*
> (Chen)

Here, we are reminded that difference is not an obstacle to harmony but its condition. In practical terms, this means embracing diverse perspectives, learning styles, and values, as well as various cultural expressions. The challenge is not to erase these differences but to align them toward a shared purpose.

In organizations, this might mean creating collaborative cultures where dissent is welcomed as part of the process. In civic life, it might mean designing dialogue that moves beyond debate into mutual exploration. In personal relationships, it means respecting the autonomy of the other while maintaining a connection. The skill is not agreement but resonance. So how do we put social harmony into action?

. . .

Practices for Cultivating Social Harmony

Social harmony does not arise by accident. It is the result of intentional habits, mindful communication, and a willingness to adapt in the face of difference. In a world of competing interests and diverse perspectives, cultivating harmony means learning how to align without forcing, to collaborate without erasing individuality. The following practices offer concrete ways to foster trust, ease tension, and create conditions where relationships — whether personal, professional, or communal — can thrive.

1. Regular Check-ins

In any ongoing relationship, whether personal or professional, regular check-ins help prevent minor frictions from escalating into larger conflicts. These can be as simple as asking, "How are we doing?" or "Is anything getting in the way of our collaboration?"

2. Perspective-Taking

Make it a habit to reflect on how a situation might feel from the other person's point of view. This builds empathy and softens defensiveness.

. . .

3. Boundary Awareness

Harmony does not mean saying yes to everything. Knowing your own limits and expressing them clearly and kindly prevents resentment.

4. Rituals of Appreciation

Small acts of gratitude can shift the emotional tone of a group. Acknowledging others' contributions, celebrating small wins, and recognizing effort foster a positive atmosphere.

5. Conflict as Opportunity

When conflict arises, treat it as a moment for growth. Approach it with the question: What is this tension revealing about our needs, assumptions, or communication?

The Goal of Social Harmony

The goal is not perfection or eternal peace. Conflict will arise. Misunderstandings will happen. But a society or group that values harmony does not panic in the face of disruption. It has the tools to restore balance. It understands that every social moment is a constellation of co-dependent factors — each person bringing their history, emotions, and needs into a shared field.

From the Daoist perspective, social harmony is not

enforced from above. It emerges from within, from each person embodying presence, responsiveness, and care. When we live with this awareness, our communities become more resilient, more humane, and more alive. We do not force unity; we cultivate it by how we show up, listen, and adapt. In the Way of Kinship, harmony is not the absence of conflict but the presence of mutual regard.

CULTIVATING ENVIRONMENTAL HARMONY

Cultivating environmental harmony is the natural extension of inner and social harmony. If we have learned to bring balance to our emotions and relationships, the next layer of this integrated worldview is our relationship with the broader living world. Daoist philosophy, particularly as presented in the Daodejing, provides a profound guide for living in harmony with nature. It teaches us to observe, adapt, and act with minimal interference. The goal is not to dominate or extract from the world but to participate in its patterns, to find our place within the flow, and to minimize resistance and disruption.

Modern life has, in many ways, separated us from this flow. Industrialization, urbanization, and a consumer economy have encouraged us to treat the environment as a collection of resources to be exploited rather than as a living network in which we are embedded. This disconnect creates disharmony, not just ecologically but psychologically and spiritually. We suffer when we cannot feel our belonging in the larger whole. Environmental crises are not just technical problems to be solved but symptoms of a deeper misalignment between human behavior and natural rhythms. A failure to recognize our co-dependence with the whole — oneness.

The Daodejing encourages us to look at the patterns of nature as the guide for right living. Environmental harmony begins by adopting the perspective of oneness. Rather than imposing our will, we seek to understand the ecosystems we inhabit and find ways to support their vitality while meeting our needs.

Environmental harmony requires observation. This involves learning about the local climate, soil, native species, and prevailing weather patterns. It means understanding seasonal shifts and the interdependencies between species. Agriculture, for instance, becomes more than food production; it becomes a practice of listening to the land and adjusting methods to preserve biodiversity and soil health. Permaculture, regenerative farming, and other sustainable practices exemplify how the principles of attention and adaptability, key Daoist virtues, can be applied to environmental stewardship.

Sometimes, action is required to restore balance. Just as inner harmony may require reframing thoughts or calming the nervous system, and social harmony may require a difficult but healing conversation, environmental harmony may require resisting destructive practices or investing in restoration. The guiding principle is whether the action supports the ongoing vitality of the whole. Does it allow the system to flourish?

The metaphor of the mirror, used to describe the still heart-mind, is also helpful here. When our inner mirror is clear, we can see the world as it is, not as we wish it to be. This clarity is essential in environmental decision-making. It allows us to see the long-term consequences of our actions rather than being driven by short-term gains or cultural assumptions. We begin to recognize that we are not separate from the earth but expressions of it, participants in its cycles.

Harmony with the environment also calls for humility. Human beings are a powerful species capable of reshaping entire biomes. But power without wisdom leads to imbalance. The Daoist sages are powerful precisely because they do not overreach. They act in accordance with the patterns they observe. This is the kind of leadership our environmental future requires: one that listens deeply acts with restraint, and values life in all its forms.

Modern science echoes these insights. Ecology, systems theory, and complexity science all affirm that everything is connected. Change in one part of an ecosystem ripples through the whole. Actions that ignore these connections often backfire. Monoculture farming, overfishing, deforestation, and pollution are examples of practices that disrupt the natural balance and cause long-term damage. Conversely, practices that support diversity, resilience, and regeneration promote health across the system.

Systems theory applies this same insight beyond the natural world, showing how social, economic, and technological networks function as interdependent wholes. A shift in one element—such as a change in policy, a technological innovation, or a market disruption—can cascade through the system in unexpected ways.

Complexity science takes this further, emphasizing that these systems are dynamic, adaptive, and often nonlinear. Small actions can trigger disproportionately large effects, and outcomes are difficult to predict. Both perspectives remind us that effective action requires awareness of relationships, feedback loops, and the potential for unintended consequences.

The Way of Kinship invites us to reframe our role in the environment. We are not stewards in the sense of managers overseeing a separate entity, nor are we lords of creation. We are participants, kin among kin. This perspective leads to a sense of reverence rather than control, of curiosity rather than conquest. We begin to ask different questions: not "How can I get more?" but "What is needed here?" or "How can I contribute to the flourishing of this place?"

Personal practices can support this shift. Spending time in nature, gardening, paying attention to local seasons and species, reducing consumption, and making choices aligned with sustainability are all small ways to reconnect with harmony. These actions may seem minor, but they are transformative. They align our attention, intention, and behavior with the living world.

Collectively, we can advocate for policies and systems that embody Daoist principles of minimal interference, long-term thinking, and valuing the whole over parts. Urban design that prioritizes green space, public transportation that reduces emissions, laws that protect biodiversity, and education that fosters ecological literacy are all expressions of a worldview that sees nature not as other but as self.

Ultimately, environmental harmony is not a separate task from inner or social harmony. All are facets of the same process of alignment. By living in accordance with the patterns of the Dao, we restore a sense of meaning, connection, and vitality to our lives. We rediscover that we are not aliens on this planet, but its expression. To care for the earth is to care for ourselves. Harmony is not a static state but an ongoing dance of seeing, adjusting, responding, and revering the living world that holds us all.

RESTORING LOST HARMONY

Harmony, as we have explored, is not a static condition but a dynamic process. Inner, social, and environmental harmony all require continual attention, adaptability, and participation. Yet, life inevitably includes conflict, rupture, and imbalance. The world is filled with injustice, suffering, and abuse. A Daoist approach does not deny this. To restore harmony when it is lost, we must begin with clarity.

1. Clarity Before Action

The first step in restoring harmony is to perceive without distortion. Emotional reactions, particularly righteous anger, can cloud understanding and lead to further disarray. The Daodejing warns that acting from a place of moral superiority often intensifies division rather than resolves it. Chapter 57 illustrates this insight:

The more prohibitions and rules,
The poor, the people become.
The sharper people's weapons,
The more they riot.
The more skilled their techniques,
The more grotesque their works.
The more elaborate the laws,
The more they commit crimes.
(Addiss & Lombardo)

This is not a call for anarchy but a warning that reactive solutions often feed the very problems they intend to solve. A Daoist response begins with slowing down, observing, and discerning the whole pattern at play — what forces, conditions, and relationships have led to the current state of disorder. This is especially important in complex or volatile situations, where apparent solutions may only scratch the surface of the problem.

Restoring harmony, then, begins with clarity: a clear mirror of the mind, undistorted by expectation, ideology, or emotional bias.

2. Transform, Don't Confront

Once clarity is established, the next step is action, but not any action. The principle of wuwei (non-coercive action) calls for a response that aligns with the underlying patterns of the situation. Wuwei is a refusal to impose artificial control or force. It encourages actions that harmonize with the situation's natural flow, nudging it back into balance.

Consider a case of workplace harassment. A typical response might be to punish the abuser. A Daoist-informed approach would begin with removing the victim from harm and then examining the structures and incentives that allowed the abuse to occur. The system would be reshaped — perhaps by creating more transparent communication channels, empowering those who were silenced, and modeling new patterns of leadership.

This transformation is not about defeating one person but about healing the context. Just as water does not shatter a rock but slowly shapes it, so too does Daoist action seek lasting change by transforming the environment.

3. Systemic Insight Over Personal Blame

A core feature of Daoist thinking is systemic awareness. Harm rarely arises from isolated acts. It is the result of disconnection, imbalance, and distortion in the larger system. Addressing injustice, then, requires working not only on the visible symptoms but on the underlying network of causes.

This systemic awareness is rooted in the Dao itself, which the Daodejing describes as the ever-present source and sustainer of all things. By observing how the Dao operates — supporting life without control, giving without claiming, and holding all within its flow—we are invited to model our actions on this pattern of unobtrusive yet life-giving influence.

The great [D]ao flows unobstructed in every
  direction.
All things rely on it to conceive and be born,
and it does not deny even the smallest of
  creation.
When it has accomplished great wonders,
it does not claim them for itself.
It nourishes infinite worlds,
yet it does not seek to master the smallest creature.
(Chapter 34, McDonald)

The idea is not to fix a person but to restore flow. When flow is blocked, violence, oppression, and confusion arise. When flow is restored, vitality and clarity return. This perspective shifts our focus from punishment to nourishment, from control to care.

For instance, in addressing systemic racism, a Daoist would look not just at changing laws but at shifting the narratives, symbols, and institutions that uphold division. Education, cultural understanding, and storytelling become tools of transformation.

4. Protect the Vulnerable

Although Daoism eschews moral dogma, it deeply values the soft, receptive, and nurturing aspects. The image of the mother, the valley, or water symbolizes this strength. Protecting the vulnerable is not a detour from Daoist values; it is their application in the human world.

This means ensuring safety, dignity, and healing for those who have been harmed. But it also means doing so in ways that do not simply create new victims or perpetuate cycles of aggression. It is a balance of assertiveness and compassion.

Repay injury with De.
(Chapter 63, Pepper & Wang)

De is not moral superiority. It is the unimpeded expression of Dao — the capacity to respond in ways that restore connection rather than deepen alienation.

5. Compassion Without Naïveté

Compassion, for the Daoist, is not soft sentimentality. It is the courageous willingness to stay open to suffering without becoming consumed by it. It includes boundaries, discernment, and skill.

In cases of domestic violence, for example, safety must be immediate. However, beyond emergency intervention, the Daoist approach examines cycles of trauma, historical disconnection, and emotional illiteracy. The response is not only extraction but transformation — through community healing, emotional education, and sustainable reconnection.

Compassion also extends to those who cause harm, not to excuse but to understand. This stance acknowledges that cruelty often stems from unresolved pain, fear, or confusion.

Addressing these root causes is essential for restoring harmony.

Restoring Harmony in Practice

Let's take a closer look at how these principles work in practical settings. In the following three scenarios, we can see brief examples from everyday life.

Scenario 1: Workplace Abuse
Instead of launching a confrontational campaign, the Daoist response begins by supporting the harmed individual without drama. Attention is paid to the culture that enabled the abuse. Conversations with leadership, invitations to more inclusive practices, and feedback mechanisms are introduced. The aim is to shift the conditions, not just replace the actors.

Scenario 2: Systemic Injustice
Rather than polarizing movements, the Daoist organizer creates spaces for connection, such as intergroup dialogues, shared projects, and media that humanize rather than demonize. The action is still political, but it is not about dominance; it is about repair.

. . .

Scenario 3: Personal Abuse or Neglect

Immediate boundaries are set. The person is removed from danger. But over time, the goal is not just to escape but to heal through practices that reconnect them to their own worth, to others, and to the flow of life.

In each of these examples, action is taken, but in a way that does not fracture the situation further. The image is of water that restores the garden, not fire that consumes it.

Harmony Is a Direction, Not a Destination

One of the most profound insights of the Daodejing is that harmony is not a fixed state but an ongoing movement. Loss of harmony is inevitable. But so is the possibility of its return. The sage does not despair over the world's disorder but walks gently and patiently, restoring connection where possible and holding stillness where not.

We do not restore harmony by force. We achieve this through perception, responsiveness, and transformation. And that begins with us: with our own mirror, our own heart, and our capacity to see clearly and act wisely.

Injustice does not call for domination. It calls for discernment. The wounds of the world will not be healed by anger alone but by the steady hands of those who are willing to see what is broken and, quietly, persistently participate in its repair.

As Chapter 78 reminds us:

> *Nothing in the world is soft and weak as water.*
> *But when attacking the hard and strong*
> *Nothing can conquer so easily.*
> *Weak overcomes strong,*
> *Soft overcomes hard.*
> *(Addiss & Lombardo)*

So, too, does harmony return — not with thunder, but with rain.

CHAPTER 12

RIGHT AND WRONG?

As we've seen, harmony — whether internal, social, or environmental — arises from responsiveness to the dynamic and interconnected nature of reality. The principles we've explored so far — interdependence, co-dependent origination, co-action, and impermanence — suggest that every situation is a confluence of countless influences, each shaping the possibilities of the moment. In such a world, nothing arises in isolation, and no action is wholly one's own. Everything we do is entangled in the patterns of life that precede and surround us. This has profound implications not only for how we act but also for how we judge actions — our own and others'.

This naturally leads us to the question of morality. If we live in a world shaped by co-arising forces and only ever understand it through partial knowledge, then what does it mean to say something is right or wrong? How do we assess responsibility, assign praise or blame, or uphold values without slipping into rigid moralism or ethical relativism? Can morality itself be reimagined in light of the Dao — as a way of being attuned rather than a fixed code? These questions do not have easy answers, but they invite us to rethink what it means to live well with others in a world where we are not separate selves but expressions of one vast unfolding pattern. This section will explore these questions.

To meaningfully explore what morality might look like in light of interdependence, co-action, and determinism, we must begin by understanding the two primary ways of speaking about morality — what we can call the outside view and the inside view. These perspectives shape not only how we define morality but also how we engage with it, whether as observers of human behavior or as participants within a moral framework.

The outside view is the descriptive approach. It treats morality as a human phenomenon — a set of social norms, customs, and expectations that arise within particular communities. From this standpoint, morality is inherently cultural and historically contingent. What is considered right or wrong, virtuous or shameful, varies from one society to another and evolves over time. This view sees morality as a product of human development, shaped by language, power structures, religious traditions, economic needs, and collective identity. In this framework, morality is not fixed or universal; it is constructed and subject to change. We can observe it, critique it, compare it across cultures, and even manipulate it — but we do so as analysts, not as believers.

For an example of the outside view of morality, consider a culture where, in one culture, euthanasia for terminally ill patients is viewed as a compassionate moral choice — an act of mercy that respects personal dignity and relieves unnecessary suffering. In another culture, the very same act is seen as deeply immoral, violating the sanctity of life and the duty to preserve it at all costs. What one community celebrates as kindness, another condemns as harm, revealing how moral judgment depends not only on the action itself but on the cultural framework in which it is interpreted.

The inside view, by contrast, is prescriptive. It is the perspective we inhabit when we treat morality not as a social convention but as something inherently true and binding. From the inside, moral values are not suggestions or customs — they are authoritative. They tell us what we should or should not do, regardless of whether others agree or whether it is advantageous. This is the moral voice we hear within ourselves when we say, "That is wrong," and mean it in a deep, non-negotiable way. It is the force that compels us to act or refrain from acting, even when it is inconvenient or dangerous to do so. In this view, morality presents itself as objective, as something that judges all values, not something to be judged.

When we hold a moral belief from the inside view — as something objectively true and authoritative — it becomes part of how we see the world and our place in it. Morality, from this perspective, is not just a social custom or personal preference. It feels like truth. So when we encounter cultures or historical periods that embrace moral norms radically different from our own, we often respond in one of two ways: we either begin to question the universality of our own moral convictions, or we double down and judge the other system as mistaken, dangerous, or even evil.

Take honor killings, for example. From the inside view of most contemporary liberal societies, the idea that someone could be morally obligated to kill a family member to preserve family honor is incomprehensible and abhorrent. Such an act violates the core values of individual rights and bodily autonomy. And yet, in some cultural contexts, honor killings are not seen as crimes but as necessary restorations of dignity. When faced with this contradiction, some may pause to reflect on how moral frameworks can diverge so completely, leading to a deeper appreciation of the contextual nature of morality. But more often, the reaction is to judge — to see the other moral system as morally inferior or even barbaric. The outsider becomes not just different but wrong.

The historical case of slavery also illustrates this pattern. Today, slavery is nearly universally condemned. But for millennia, it was a foundational institution defended by religion, philosophy, and law. We might be tempted to use this example to confirm the superiority of our current moral view, treating past civilizations as morally blind while assuming our own clarity. This judgment comforts us. It spares us from having to ask the more unsettling question: if they could be wrong and not know it, could we be wrong and not know it?

These examples show that while encountering moral diversity can be an opportunity to reflect on the contingent and constructed nature of our moral views, it often becomes a stage for reaffirming our insider commitments and judging others. This tension lies at the heart of cross-cultural and historical moral reflection. Do we allow ourselves to be changed, or do we use the immoral "other" to reinforce what we already believe?

Understanding this dynamic is crucial for exploring morality in light of interdependence, co-action, determinism, and limited knowledge. If we recognize that every moral judgment arises from a particular position — socially, historically, psychologically — we can begin to approach morality with more humility and curiosity, without necessarily surrendering our values. But we must also be honest about how often we resort to judgment over understanding. This habit, too, is part of the moral landscape we inhabit.

Morality functions as a powerful mechanism for enforcing social conformity. When moral norms are internalized as universal and unquestionable truths, they exert immense pressure on individuals to align with the expectations of their community. But what often goes unnoticed is how these norms may serve interests beyond the well-being or flourishing of individuals. They can reflect the power dynamics, economic priorities, or cultural anxieties of a society, even while appearing as noble or self-evident truths.

For example, moral prohibitions on certain forms of sexuality have often been justified as preserving virtue, tradition, or divine order. Yet behind those justifications are frequent concerns about controlling reproduction, inheritance, or maintaining patriarchal authority. When such moral rules are presented as unquestionable goods, dissenters are not just viewed as different but as immoral. The moral system becomes a tool for marginalizing alternative ways of living that threaten dominant structures.

This is particularly visible when morality is invoked to justify the status quo. For instance, norms around hard work, individual responsibility, and self-reliance are often treated as moral imperatives in capitalist societies. These values can serve to obscure structural inequalities by placing moral blame on individuals who fail to thrive. Poverty becomes a sign of moral failing, not a symptom of systemic imbalance. In this way, morality doesn't just guide behavior; it conceals the workings of power and naturalizes the outcomes of unjust systems.

When morality functions in this way, it no longer merely encourages social cooperation; it becomes a gatekeeping tool and a bully stick. Those who conform are rewarded with legitimacy and acceptance. Those who question the norms or are unable to live by them are often labeled as deviant or dangerous. The threat of being seen as immoral becomes a profoundly effective form of social control. Few things cut as deeply as moral condemnation. This makes morality a potent force, not only for guiding individual behavior but also for maintaining collective cohesion and silencing dissent.

Of course, this isn't to say that all moral norms are

cynical or manipulative. Many arise from genuine attempts to foster compassion, fairness, and mutual care. But even well-intentioned moral systems can carry embedded assumptions and hidden interests, especially when the morality cannot be questioned. The outsider view might encourage us to ask: Who benefits from this particular moral judgment? What patterns are being reinforced or disrupted? And can we distinguish the call for harmony from the demand for conformity?

One of the deepest challenges in the realm of morality is the danger of hubris — the overconfidence that we know what is right, true, and good in an ultimate sense. This confidence can be both seductive and socially reinforced. When a moral position is held as unquestionably correct, dissent or alternative views are not merely seen as different but as threats to truth, to decency, to civilization itself. And yet, the history of moral thought, across cultures and centuries, is a long record of change, reversal, and contradiction. What one age holds as sacred, another sees as cruel. What one culture praises as virtuous, another condemns as oppressive.

The problem is not simply that we make moral mistakes — it is that we often don't recognize them as mistakes until long after the fact. This delay is rooted in the illusion of moral certainty. We assume that our moral frameworks are based on sound reasoning, divine revelation, or the obvious requirements of human well-being. However, these frameworks are always filtered through limited knowledge, personal bias, social conditioning, and emotional attachment. When we believe too strongly in the infallibility of our moral vision, we stop asking questions. We stop listening. And we become blind to the ways our actions might be causing harm under the banner of doing good.

Overconfidence in moral judgment also hinders learning and adaptation. If we are convinced we already possess the right values, we resist evidence or experience that challenges them. We may double down instead of reevaluating and defend instead of rethinking. In this sense, moral hubris hinders growth — both personal and social. It becomes not just an obstacle to understanding others but a block to understanding ourselves.

The danger is magnified when moral certainty is institutionalized — codified into laws, wielded by governments, or taught as unquestionable doctrine. Here, overconfidence becomes not just a personal failing but a systemic one. It can justify violence, exclusion, and injustice — all while claiming the highest moral ground. History gives us chilling examples of this, from religious inquisitions to cultural genocides to ideological purges. In each case, certainty in moral righteousness was used to silence doubt and legitimize cruelty.

The perspective of oneness warns against such overreach. It reminds us that knowledge is always partial, that reality is fluid, and that the patterns we grasp are never the whole of things. What are we to do then, give up on morality? Yes! This concept is called amorality.

· · ·

Amorality refers to the absence or rejection of moral judgments, standards, or considerations. An amoral perspective does not distinguish between right and wrong in the moral sense, not because it endorses immorality but because it operates outside the framework of morality altogether. Amorality is a deliberate philosophical stance — the view that concepts like "good" and "evil" are human inventions and lack objective grounding. In contrast to the insider view of morality, where moral truths are experienced as binding and real, the amoral stance treats morality as a social construct, one that is descriptive rather than prescriptive. Importantly, amorality does not necessarily lead to harmful behavior; instead, it reframes ethical action as a matter of preference, consequence, or systemic design rather than moral obligation.

From the perspective of amorality, a society need not rely on the assumption of objective moral truths to function effectively or compassionately. Within an amoral framework, communities can still cultivate and uphold laws and shared values — such as fairness, cooperation, safety, or mutual respect — as guiding principles. The key difference is that these values are understood to be socially constructed, not absolute. Because of this, they are inherently open to examination, justification, and revision.

Rather than being enforced as unquestionable truths, such values are treated as evolving agreements — tools that help communities function well in a given context. Their legitimacy comes not from divine authority or rational certainty but from their effectiveness in fostering well-being, reducing harm, or creating a desired way of living together. This perspective encourages transparency about why certain norms are promoted and who benefits from them. It also invites humility since no one can claim final knowledge of what is "right" for all people in all circumstances.

Importantly, when values are acknowledged as subjective, the conversation shifts from moral condemnation to critical dialogue. Instead of declaring one's culture or beliefs morally superior, people can engage with others about the consequences of actions, the needs being met or unmet, and the possibility of alternatives. This opens the door to developing values, not as a quest for absolute answers but as a continuous process of shared learning and adaptation.

The Way of Kinship proceeds from an amoral perspective, offering a path grounded not in rigid moral absolutes but in lived responsiveness to the interconnected web of existence. Rather than seeking to anchor life in universal commandments or eternal truths, it invites us to attune ourselves to the ever-changing, co-arising conditions of each moment, guided by clarity, compassion, and adaptability. It does not reject values but reorients them as tools for harmony rather than weapons of judgment. By recognizing that our ideals are born of our context — not imposed by some transcendent source — we gain the freedom to reshape them with humility, creativity, and care. In this way, the Way of Kinship becomes a practice of belonging: not through conformity, but through conscious participation in the unfolding process of life.

CHAPTER 13
GOVERNMENT

When we are genuinely concerned about human well-being, it is not enough to focus solely on the individual; we must also consider the broader social context. Humans are inherently social creatures — our lives are shaped by the networks, institutions, and systems in which we are embedded. Chief among these is government, the formal structure through which collective decisions are made, resources are allocated, and social order is maintained. Politics, broadly understood, is the process by which power is distributed and wielded in these systems. To ignore politics is to overlook a significant force that determines who thrives and who struggles, who is protected, and who is vulnerable.

Even the most personal aspects of life — access to clean air and water, education, healthcare, security, and freedom — are deeply political. They depend on policies, funding, and the values enshrined in laws and leadership. Individual practices of mindfulness, compassion, or ethical living are essential. Still, they do not replace the need to engage with the structures that influence the lives of millions. Addressing government is not about partisanship or ideology; it is about recognizing that systems of power either support or erode human flourishing. If we genuinely care about well-being — not just our own but that of our communities and future generations — we must concern ourselves with how power is organized, who it serves, and how it can be made more just, responsive, and life-affirming.

Many readers are surprised to discover how much of the Daodejing is devoted to the subject of government and leadership. Popular portrayals often present the text as a mystical manual for personal peace or spiritual insight, emphasizing self-cultivation, inner harmony, and alignment with nature. And while those themes are certainly present, they coexist with a sustained focus on governing wisely and humanely. Far from being an apolitical text, the Daodejing speaks repeatedly about rulers, governance, laws, and the well-being of the people.

This focus surprises modern readers because we often separate the inner life from political life, imagining that one can pursue personal wisdom without engaging with social systems. But the Daodejing reflects a different worldview — one grounded in interdependence. From this perspective, the way we govern and the way we live are deeply connected. Human well-being cannot be disentangled from the structures of power that shape our world. Thus, the sage's wisdom is not just inward but also social and political. The same principles that guide harmonious living — humility, restraint, attentiveness to natural patterns, and non-coercive influence — are also the principles that guide just governance.

The surprise, then, comes not from the presence of politics in the Daodejing but from our cultural expectation that spiritual texts should remain private and apolitical. In contrast, the Daodejing's vision challenges us to see leadership itself as a spiritual discipline — one that either aligns with the Dao and nourishes life or deviates from it and produces suffering.

The Daodejing provides several poignant examples of how rulers or governments fail their people through overreach, pride, and reliance on coercion. It critiques the very patterns of governance that many societies, ancient and modern, take for granted: the proliferation of laws, the display of wealth, the use of force, and the pursuit of moralistic control.

One of the clearest examples comes from Chapter 57, where the consequences of excessive governance are laid out plainly:

> *The more prohibitions and rules,*
> *The poor, the people become.*
> *The sharper people's weapons,*
> *The more they riot.*
> *The more skilled their techniques,*
> *The more grotesque their works.*

The more elaborate the laws,
The more they commit crimes.
(Addiss & Lombardo)

This passage critiques a government that tries to secure order through restrictions, military buildup, and excessive legislation. Rather than creating safety and prosperity, these efforts generate poverty, unrest, and criminality. The failure here is not negligence but excess, trying to control society rather than nourish it.

Chapter 75 gives a more explicit diagnosis of poor leadership:

Why are the people starving?
Because the rulers eat up the money in taxes.
Therefore the people are starving.

Why are the people rebellious?
Because the rulers interfere too much.
Therefore the people are rebellious.

Why do the people think so little of death?
Because the rulers demand too much of life.
Therefore the people take death lightly.

Having little to live on, they know better than
to value life too highly.
(Feng & English)

Here, the suffering of the people is directly linked to the failures of leadership, including over-taxation, over-intervention, and excessive demands. The sage is pointing to a government that burdens rather than supports and, in doing so, creates the very chaos it seeks to suppress.

Chapter 53 contrasts the path of the Dao with the indulgent lifestyles of corrupt rulers:

> *The great Way [Dao] is smooth and easy;*
> *Yet people love to take shortcuts!*
> *The court is resplendent;*
> *Yet the fields are overgrown.*
> *The granaries are empty;*
> *Yet some wear elegant clothes;*
> *Fine swords dangle at their sides;*
> *They are stuffed with food and drink;*
> *And possess wealth in gross abundance.*
> *This is known as taking pride in robbery.*
> *(Ivanhoe)*

This passage portrays a government obsessed with displays of power and luxury while neglecting the land and the common people. The court's extravagance is called what it is: robbery. When rulers enrich themselves at the expense of the people, they have strayed far from the Dao.

These passages illustrate a Daoist diagnosis of political failure rooted in disconnection: from the people, from simplicity, and from the natural order. When rulers grasp, control, and moralize, they sow disorder. When they listen, observe, and let the Dao guide their actions, harmony is possible. The ideal ruler in the Daodejing does not impose their will through force or rigid law but leads in a nearly invisible way, cultivating conditions in which the people flourish on their own.

The sentence "The best leaders are those the people hardly know exist" (McDonald, Chapter 17) recognizes that imposing rigid controls often backfires, generating resistance, resentment, and disorder. Instead, the Daodejing teaches that harmony arises when a ruler refrains from micromanaging, avoids self-aggrandizement, and governs in accordance with the rhythms and needs of the people. The sage-ruler acts through wuwei (non-coercive action), letting things unfold naturally while gently guiding from behind the scenes.

Rulers are also warned against pride, aggression, and the accumulation of weapons or wealth: "Ruling the country is like cooking a small fish." (Feng & English, Chapter 60) The more a leader interferes, the greater the imbalance introduced. Instead, the Daodejing suggests that soft and yielding approaches often achieve more than forceful ones: "Weak overcomes strong, Soft overcomes hard." (Addiss & Lombardo, Chapter 78)

In short, the Daodejing envisions rulership as a form of deep wisdom practice. Good governance is not about enforcing morality or shaping society to an ideal. It is about aligning with the Dao, nurturing what is already present, and allowing the people to live with dignity, simplicity, and freedom. It's a vision that sees political leadership not as a tool for control but as a subtle art of facilitation, where the greatest success leaves no trace of the ruler's hand.

RETURNING TO 樸 (PǓ): THE UNTAMED INTEGRITY OF BEING

One of the most evocative concepts in the Daodejing is 樸 (pǔ), often translated as "the uncarved block." The image evokes raw wood—natural, untouched, and whole. Yet the English term "uncarved block" has long puzzled readers. After all, a block is already shaped, squared off, and measured. It suggests planning, utility, and transformation — all the marks of human intervention. In Daoist thought, however, 樸 (pǔ) refers to the pre-carved state not yet molded by agendas or roles. It is the original condition of things before culture shapes them into conformity.

Applied to human life, 樸 (pǔ) represents a person's natural state before being cut, polished, or chiseled into the social roles prescribed by family, tradition, and government. In contrast to the Confucian vision of virtue cultivated through ritual, hierarchy, and adherence to tradition, the Daoist value of 樸 (pǔ) emphasizes spontaneity, wholeness, and resistance to premature definition. Confucianism assumes that virtue comes from carving people into shapes that fit the larger social puzzle. Daoism sees this as a tragic misunderstanding of human nature and a source of social unrest.

This critique emerges subtly yet sharply in the Daodejing. Consider Chapter 28:

Be familiar with what is pure and white
But watch over what is dark and black —
And become the Pattern for the World ...

Turn back to being an Uncarved Block [樸 pǔ].
When the Uncarved Block is cut up
then it becomes a government tool.
When the Wise Person instead uses it
then it becomes head of the government.
Yes:
A great carver does no cutting,
A great ruler makes no rules.
(LaFargue)

Here, the text encourages holding both awareness and humility—symbolized by "white" and "black"—to become a model for others. But the ideal is not dominance or performance; it is returning to 樸, a state prior to social distinction. The phrase implies that wisdom lies not in becoming something else but in undoing what has been layered on.

Daoist philosophy emerged during the Warring States period — a time of immense political upheaval, constant warfare, and competing doctrines on how to restore order. Confucianism promoted a highly structured society where each person had a defined role, such as ruler, subject, father, son, elder, or youth. These roles came with rituals, duties, and expectations. But Daoism saw in this system a kind of violent overreach — an attempt to carve people into rigid shapes that served the powerful but stifled the human spirit.

Chapter 32 reflects this tension:

> *Once the whole is divided, the parts need*
> > *names.*
> *There are already enough names.*
> *We need to know when to stop.*
> *Knowing when to stop averts trouble.*
> *Tao in the world is like a river flowing home to*
> > *the sea.*
> *(Feng & English)*

This passage alludes to the moment when natural wholeness (Dao) gets carved into conceptual categories and roles. Naming, defining, and dividing are all forms of "carving." While necessary in limited ways, they become dangerous when taken as absolute. When people are forced into names they do not choose, they chafe. And when this pressure becomes too great, they rebel.

Indeed, a subtle reading of the Daodejing presents the chaos of the Warring States not merely as a failure of governance but as the inevitable backlash against systems that tried to slice humanity into unnatural shapes. People who resist their assigned roles are not broken — they are alive. Daoism asks: What if the solution to social disorder isn't more structure, more hierarchy, more carving — but less?

Chapter 37 offers a powerful summary of this vision:

> *The Dao is constantly without action [wuwei],*
>   *and yet it leaves nothing undone.*
> *If nobles and kings are able to guard it, the*
>   *myriad beings will naturally transform.*
> *In transformation, desires may arise; I will calm*
>   *them through nameless unhewn simplicity*
>   *[樸 pǔ].*
> *Through this nameless unhewn simplicity,*
> *I will become desireless.*
> *Being desireless through stillness,*
> *The world will become naturally settled.*
> *(Komjathy)*

Here, we see the essence of 樸 (pǔ): a political and social ethic that doesn't suppress natural diversity but allows it to emerge and harmonize on its own. The role of the sage (or ruler) is not to mold people into compliance but to create conditions where their natural goodness (德 dé) can flow without coercion. The uncarved life is not chaotic; it is integrated. It follows patterns without enforcing them.

To return to 樸 (pǔ) is not to abandon society but to reimagine it. It is to let go of the illusion that control equals harmony and to recognize that genuine stability arises from mutual responsiveness. A society that upholds 樸 (pǔ) does not hammer its people into order; it listens, watches, and adapts. It trusts the living intelligence of the whole.

In this light, 樸 (pǔ) is not primitive — it is mature. It is not naïve — it is wise. It asks not how to fix people but how to let them flourish without distortion. And that, the Daodejing suggests, is the deepest kind of political skill.

THE DAODEJING'S VIEW OF WAR: POWER WITHOUT WISDOM

Of all the powers a state can wield, war stands as its most severe and irreversible. It is the ultimate assertion of control — a decision that brings death, destruction, and deep social rupture. In the Daodejing, war is not glorified or celebrated. It is treated as a failure of leadership, a last resort, and a tragic departure from the harmony of the Dao. The text's warnings against war are among its most explicit condemnations of excessive action and misguided ambition.

Chapter 31 opens this critique:

> *Good weapons are instruments of fear; all*
> *   creatures hate them.*
> *Therefore followers of Tao never use them.*
> *The wise prefer the left.*
> *Soldiers prefer the right.*

> *Weapons are instruments of fear; they are not*
> *   tools of the wise.*
> *They use them only when there is no choice.*
> *Peace and quiet are dear to their hearts,*
> *And victory no cause for rejoicing.*
> *If you rejoice in victory, then you delight in*
> *   killing;*
> *If you delight in killing, you cannot fulfill*
> *   yourself.*

On happy occasions precedence is given to the
    left,
On sad occasions to the right.
In the army the general stands on the left,
The commander-in-chief on the right.
This means that war is conducted like a funeral.
When many people are killed,
They should be mourned in heartfelt sorrow.
That is why a victory must be observed like a
    funeral.
(Feng & English)

Here, the text uses a tone of solemn disapproval. Weapons, though sometimes necessary, are never good. The sage does not cling to pacifism for its own sake but sees the deeper truth: the use of force always carries consequences beyond the battlefield. Even in victory, war leaves behind resentment, grief, and cycles of retaliation. Rejoicing in violence, or seeking it out for gain or glory, is seen as a moral and spiritual deformity.

This stands in stark contrast to many traditions — ancient and modern — that celebrate war as the proving ground of virtue, honor, or destiny. In the Daoist view, war represents the loss of the natural order, a descent into imbalance. Harmony cannot be enforced at the point of a sword. To engage in war is to step outside of the Dao, and only with great caution and reluctance should it ever be done.

Chapter 69 gives us a powerful metaphor drawn from military strategy:

There is a saying in the army:
I do not presume to be the master.
But become the guest.
I do not dare advance an inch
But retreat a foot.

This is called moving without moving,
Rolling up sleeves without baring your arms,
Repelling without opposing,
Wielding without a weapon.

There is no disaster greater than
Contempt for the enemy.
Contempt for the enemy—
What a treasure lost!

Therefore,
When the fighting gets hot,
Those who grieve will conquer.
(Addiss & Lombardo)

This passage flips conventional logic on its head. Strength is found not in domination but in humility. The most effective military strategy is one that avoids battle. The best warrior is the one who carries grief, not pride. This way of thinking reflects a deep understanding of interdependence and consequence. Even just wars damage the fabric of life. They disrupt the relationships that sustain communities and environments.

To the Daoists, the root of war is not evil people but

imbalanced systems — greed, ambition, fear, and ego-driven leadership. Chapter 46 diagnoses the cause with clarity:

> *There is no greater calamity*
> *Than not knowing what is enough.*
> *There is no greater fault*
> *Than desire for success.*
>
> *Therefore,*
> *Knowing that enough is enough*
> *Is always Enough.*
> *(Addiss & Lombardo)*

Here, we see that the seeds of war are sown long before armies march. When rulers are never satisfied — when they seek expansion, conquest, or prestige — they create the conditions for violence. The antidote is not military buildup but inner stillness and governance rooted in sufficiency.

THE PROBLEM OF GLORY

Another critical theme in the Daodejing is its rejection of military glory. Victories in war, even when strategically sound or politically necessary, are not to be celebrated. Chapter 30 warns:

> *Whenever you advise rulers in the way of Tao,*
> *Counsel them not to use force to conquer the*
>   *universe.*

For this would only cause resistance.
Thorn bushes spring up wherever the army has
*   passed.*
Lean years follow in the wake of a great war.
Just do what needs to be done.
Never take advantage of power.

Achieve results,
But never glory in them.
Achieve results,
But never boast.
Achieve results,
But never be proud.
Achieve results,
Because this is the natural way.
Achieve results,
But not through violence.

Force is followed by loss of strength.
This is not the way of the Tao.
That which goes against the Tao
Comes to an early end."
(Feng & English)

In these lines, the Daodejing offers a profound ethic of restraint. Even when power is used, it should not be embraced. The sage leader acts as little as necessary and always with reluctance. To boast of killing is to show you have not understood the cost of life. The more profound message is that real power lies in restraint, in knowing when not to act.

THE ETHICS OF DEFENSE

While Daoism is critical of aggression, it is not naïve. The Daodejing acknowledges that threats may arise and that leaders have a responsibility to protect their people. However, even here, the emphasis remains on minimizing harm, avoiding escalation, and acting without self-interest. It aligns with a logic of stability, not conquest, of survival, not dominance.

In this way, Daoist governance does not forgo the use of power, but it seeks to redefine power. Authentic leadership is not found in the ability to destroy enemies but in the capacity to prevent enmity in the first place. War, when unavoidable, should be waged like surgery — reluctantly, precisely, and with full awareness of the pain it causes.

The Daodejing's approach to war is not simply about policy — it is a philosophy of life. War is the most visible rupture in the fabric of interdependence. It reflects the breakdown of communication, the failure of leadership, and the loss of harmony. For the Daoist, a world with fewer wars is not just a more peaceful world; it is a world more aligned with the Dao.

War, in this view, is not only destructive in the external sense. It also erodes the inner clarity and balance that wise leadership requires. To embrace war eagerly is to lose the path. To resist it when possible and to grieve its necessity when not is to remain close to the Way.

To walk the Way of Kinship is to recognize that harmony is not limited to personal peace, nor is it achieved through the enforcement of rigid ideals. Harmony arises when we live in respectful relationships with ourselves, others, the natural world, and the structures of governance that shape our lives. The Daodejing invites us to imagine leadership not as domination but as stewardship grounded in humility and interdependence. When rulers impose, people resist. When they listen and guide with lightness, communities flourish. This path honors the uncarved nature of people, resists the violence of unnecessary shaping, and refuses the false promise of control through force. War, hierarchy, and coercion are all signs of deviation from the Dao — they indicate that the living patterns of kinship have been forgotten. To return is not to abandon society but to renew it through presence, simplicity, and deep responsiveness. In doing so, we move toward a world in which all beings can live and thrive together in mutual unfolding. This is the wisdom of the Dao and the heart of kinship.

CHAPTER 14

LIVING BETWEEN WORLDS

W hen we begin to see life through a different lens, we do more than shift perspective. We step into another world, one that may feel more real, more humane, and more whole. But often, it is not the world we were born into.

Many people find themselves living between two worlds: the one they have come to see as true and the one that continues to dominate the structures around them. In one world, the values of kinship, attunement, and natural harmony feel obvious, even necessary. In the other, utility, status, consumption, and control continue to shape institutions, conversations, and expectations. Living between these two worlds is a lived dissonance — a challenge that affects work, relationships, time, and even one's identity.

This is the reality for those who awaken to a different way of being in a world that often does not recognize or reward it. You may feel the dissonance in your workplace, where success is measured by metrics that ignore human and ecological costs. You may feel it in your relationships, where the pace and priorities of others pull you back toward old patterns. You may feel it in the loneliness of questioning what others take for granted. To walk the Way of Kinship is, at times, to feel out of step.

This can be painful. When your sense of what matters diverges from the culture around you, even small choices can feel loaded. Choosing to move more slowly, to work less, to speak differently, to resist judgment, or to prioritize the health of the whole — these are not always legible within dominant norms. You may be seen as impractical, soft, naïve, or even threatening. The pressure to conform is rarely overt, but it is always present, working through subtle cues: praise withheld, opportunities missed, confusion or dismissal in others' eyes.

And yet, the pain of the old world — the one organized around scarcity, extraction, and individualism — is what drives many of us to seek another way in the first place. Once we have glimpsed the deeper reality of interconnection, it is difficult to return. And so we find ourselves between worlds: belonging fully to neither, yet shaped by both.

This in-between space can be fertile if we learn how to dwell in it skillfully. Here are several practices and perspectives that can help support this way of living:

1. Honor the Dissonance

First, acknowledge that the dissonance is real and a sign of your growth, not a failure. Feeling out of place is not a symptom to be fixed but a sign that your inner world is beginning to align with a more profound truth. When your values start to shift, it is natural to experience discomfort in environments that operate on a different logic. Rather than suppress this tension or try to resolve it too quickly, treat it as a teacher. What is it revealing about your needs, your limits, your longings?

You do not have to harmonize the two worlds right away. The practice is to remain faithful to what you have come to know, even when it is difficult. You are not alone in this challenge — many have walked this path, and many are walking it now.

2. Translate, Don't Preach

Living differently does not mean separating entirely from the dominant culture. In many cases, you will still have to speak its language — at work, in your family, in public life. Rather than reject the old world outright, learn to translate. Translate your values into terms that others can hear, even if they don't share your lens. Lead with curiosity rather than critique. Speak in a way that opens rather than alienates.

For example, if your workplace values productivity above all, speak about how rest and clarity increase creativity and effectiveness. If your peers value achievement, talk about the freedom and depth that come with letting go. You don't have to compromise your vision, but you may need to translate it so others can begin to sense its truth.

3. Build Community

One of the most powerful supports for living differently is to find others who share your orientation. These relationships may be rare, but they are essential. Seek out conversations that nourish you. Create rituals of presence with others. Even one or two trusted companions who hold similar values can transform the feeling of isolation into a sense of belonging.

If such a community does not yet exist around you, begin quietly. Offer space. Hold gatherings. Share what you are learning without demanding agreement. Sometimes, the most powerful communities are not built through persuasion but through resonance — people find each other because the same longing lives in them.

You don't need a large group to feel supported. Even a small, sincere circle of people who are committed to living with care, integrity, and attention can provide immense strength. Check out our community at: www.Kinship.Cafe

4. Tend to Your Inner State

When you live between worlds, your inner state becomes a kind of home. Make it a refuge. Cultivate practices that help you return to stillness and clarity. This might include meditation, time in nature, journaling, movement, or simply taking moments of silence amidst daily life. The more deeply rooted you are in your own sense of being, the less vulnerable you will be to the crosscurrents of cultural pressure.

The metaphor of the mirror pool becomes especially important here. In a world full of turbulence, your calm heart-mind becomes the means by which you see clearly and respond wisely. The ripples from the outer world may never stop, but with patience and care, you can learn to see through them.

5. Practice Micro-Resistance

Living differently does not always require grand gestures. Often, it means choosing differently in small, consistent ways. It means saying no to unnecessary busyness and yes to rest. It means valuing relationships over reputation, presence over speed, and enough over more. These choices may not make headlines, but they shape a life.

They also signal to others that another way is possible. Quiet forms of resistance — gentle refusals, reorientations, acts of kindness — are powerful because they build new patterns without seeking to dominate. Over time, these new patterns give rise to cultural alternatives.

6. Remember You Are Already Part of a Larger Shift

Finally, know that the longing you carry is not just personal. You are part of a broader movement — one that stretches across traditions, continents, and generations. There is a growing recognition, often quiet but deeply

rooted, that the dominant ways of life are unsustainable —
not just ecologically but emotionally and spiritually. The
shift toward interdependence, kinship, and care is
happening, even when it is hard to see.

When you live between worlds, you carry a thread of that
shift within you. You may not be able to see the whole
pattern yet, but you are part of its unfolding. And your
presence, your clarity, your refusal to pretend otherwise—
these are seeds for the future.

   To live in two worlds is to carry tension, yes. But it is also
to become a bridge. A witness. A quiet revolutionary. You are
not here to escape this world. You are here to help it
remember something it forgot: that life is not a competition
but a shared unfolding. That worth is not earned but
inherent. That wisdom lies not in control but in attunement.
And that, even in a fractured time, we can still live in ways
that make oneness visible.

THE PATH OF THE SAGE

T o live between worlds is to become a kind of intermediary — a person who sees through the illusions of the dominant worldview but continues to walk among those who are still shaped by it. This is not a role one claims with pride. It is a calling that emerges quietly, almost reluctantly, through the persistent desire to live in greater alignment with what one knows to be true. In the Daodejing, such a person is called a sage, not because they possess special powers, but because they see clearly and act accordingly.

The sage does not retreat into seclusion nor shout above the crowd. Instead, they embody the values of the world they know is possible, even when surrounded by a world that insists otherwise. Their power lies not in their control over others but in their refusal to be controlled by illusions. They live simply. They act without coercion. They influence without seeking attention.

The sage is not reactive, not easily swayed by praise or blame. Their strength lies in a heart that remains open, a mind that remains responsive, and a will that is not captured by ego. In modern terms, the sage lives in a state of deep integration. They do not compartmentalize ethics from emotion, or self from society, or nature from culture. Their life becomes an embodiment of oneness.

In an age of division and noise, the figure of the sage may seem distant, even unreachable. But Daoist wisdom suggests otherwise. The sage is not a superhero or prophet. The sage is someone who has stopped pretending. They have ceased striving to impress, to dominate, to accumulate. They have returned to something more fundamental, something always available: attunement to what is.

This return does not happen all at once. It is a practice — daily, quiet, often unnoticed. It begins with watching the breath, walking with attention, responding instead of reacting. It deepens with listening to the needs of the body, the emotions, the people around us, and the world itself. It matures as we begin to trust the unfolding of things, letting go of the need to impose a story, a meaning, or a control over what is not ours to command.

The sage lives in the in-between space and learns to make peace with it. They carry both the pain of knowing and the gift of remembering. They recognize that many are not yet ready to see what they see, and they respond with patience. Not everyone needs to be convinced. Not every conflict needs to be won. The sage knows that the deeper work is not always visible — that change often begins in the soil before it appears in the bloom.

Chapter 15 describes the sage through a series of metaphors:

> *The great masters of ancient times*
> *focused on the indiscernible*
> *and penetrated the dark*
> *you would never know them*
> *and because you wouldn't know them*
> *I describe them with reluctance*
> *they were careful as if crossing a river in winter*
> *cautious as if worried about neighbors*
> *reserved like a guest*
> *ephemeral like melting ice*
> *simple like uncarved wood*
> *open like a valley*
> *and murky like a puddle*
> *but those that can be like a puddle*
> *become clear when they're still."*
> *(Pine)*

Each of these images reveals not power in the conventional sense but something deeper: presence, adaptability, and trust in the Dao. The sage does not resist the currents of life, nor are they swept away by them. They move with awareness, with care, and with a deep willingness to be shaped by the moment without being deformed by it.

· · ·

This is the invitation before us. To walk the Way of Kinship is to live in recognition of the interwoven fabric of life. To become a sage is to commit to living that recognition with clarity and compassion. You do not need to renounce the world. You do not need to become perfect. You need only to begin returning to what is simple, to what is real, to what calls you beyond the noise.

To live this way is not to escape the old world but to plant seeds of the new one — quietly, persistently, in the soil of your own life. And from those seeds, new patterns will emerge. Some will blossom in your time. Others may not. But the sage does not measure their life by results. They measure it by fidelity to the Way.

In the end, you may still find yourself between worlds. But you will not be alone. And in time, others will find you, not because you told them the way, but because you became it.

CHAPTER 16

DEATH AND THE WAY OF KINSHIP

I was born together with heaven and earth, so
the ten thousand things and I are one and
the same.
(Zhuangzi, Chapter 2, Hinton)

Among all the realities of existence, death is the one that most definitively shapes the contours of life. It is the boundary that gives our experiences their urgency, poignancy, and meaning. From the moment we are born, death is with us — not as an enemy, but as a companion that reminds us that life is finite, precious, and shared. The Way of Kinship, grounded in both the naturalism of the Daodejing and a contemporary scientific understanding of life, offers a perspective that invites us not to fear death but to see it as an integral part of the great unfolding of existence.

The Daodejing does not dwell on death in the sense of personal grief or existential dread. It does not provide promises of an afterlife or warnings of divine judgment. Instead, it speaks to the patterns of nature, where birth and death are part of the same movement. Chapter 16 offers one of the clearest reflections on this:

> *The ten thousand things rise and fall while the*
> *self watches their return.*
> *They grow and flourish and then return to the*
> *source.*
> *Returning to the source is stillness, which is the*
> *way of nature.*
> *The way of nature is unchanging."*
> *(Feng & English)*

In this view, death is not an aberration but a return to the source, to the quiet mystery out of which all things arise and into which all things dissolve. To fear death, then, is to misunderstand life. What arises must return. What lives must die. What is born into form must eventually return to formlessness. The cycle is not tragic; it is the very shape of the Dao.

From the standpoint of philosophical naturalism, this insight finds further grounding. Evolutionary biology tells us that life as we know it depends on death. Without death, there would be no room for new life, no turnover of generations, and no opportunity for adaptation and growth. Death is the gift that one generation gives to the next, allowing new ideas, bodies, and relationships to emerge. Without the limit of death, life would stagnate. Leadership would calcify, creativity would wane, and our world would become frozen in time.

To embrace death is to embrace change. It is to recognize that we are part of a vast, interdependent web of becoming. Our lives are not separate entities but moments in a great conversation — expressions of the Dao as it unfolds through time. Just as leaves fall in autumn to nourish the soil for spring, so too do our lives nourish the lives to come.

This is why the Daodejing so often praises stillness, emptiness, and yielding. These are not deathly qualities in the morbid sense but invitations to let go of grasping and control. In letting go, we align ourselves with the Dao. We accept the passage of time, the erosion of identity, and the eventual dissolution of the self not as failures but as the very fabric of reality. Chapter 22 says:

> *To yield is to be preserved whole.*
> *To be bent is to become straight.*
> *To be hollow is to be filled.*
> *(Yutang)*

We can see in these lines a profound wisdom about mortality. In letting go of permanence, we gain peace. In yielding to the reality of death, we discover a kind of continuity that is independent of individual survival. We become part of a larger pattern, one that existed long before us and will continue long after.

The Western philosophical tradition often approaches death with fear or resistance. Much of modern culture is built on the denial of death: our endless striving for productivity, youthfulness, and legacy can be seen as attempts to escape our impermanence. But the naturalistic perspective, like the Daoist, offers a different path. It invites us to face death squarely, not with resignation but with reverence. Death gives our life its shape. It reminds us that our choices matter, that our relationships are limited in time, and that our presence here is a privilege.

From this view, immortality is not a gift but a danger. Immortality would erase the very distinctions that give life meaning. Without the boundary of death, there would be no urgency to act, no reason to cherish a moment, and no end to selfish accumulation. Immortality would not liberate us; it would unmoor us from the rhythms of existence that ground us in empathy, humility, and awe.

Living in the shadow of death, then, is not a curse. It is a call to awaken. Each moment becomes more vibrant when we realize it will pass. Each relationship becomes more sacred when we understand it is finite. The Daodejing teaches that those who understand the Dao do not cling to it. They do not resist change. They flow with the world, not against it. Those who accept death live without illusion. They are not paralyzed by fear. They do not build their identities around permanence. Instead, they live lightly, generously, and in tune with the ephemeral nature of all things.

One might ask: But what of grief? What of the pain of losing someone we love? The Daoist response is not to dismiss grief but to place it within a larger context. Grief is not a sign of failure; it is a sign of connection. We grieve because we have loved, because our lives have been shaped by others, and because their absence creates a real ache. But even grief, like everything else, moves in cycles. It comes, it transforms, and it returns us — if we let it — to a deeper appreciation of life.

To grieve in alignment with the Dao is not to wallow or to deny. It is to allow the process of mourning to unfold without resistance. It is to honor the life that was lived, to acknowledge our sorrow, and to remain open to the beauty that continues. The mirror-pool metaphor from Daoist thought is relevant here: when the heart-mind is calm, it reflects clearly. When it is disturbed, the world becomes distorted. Grief can stir the waters, but with time and compassion, the stillness returns.

This is not a suppression of emotion. It is a dynamic equilibrium, a way of holding even our sorrow lightly as part of the dance of life and death. Chapter 76 reminds us:

> *We are born gentle and weak, but at death are*
> *stiff and hard.*
> *Green plants are tender and filled with sap.*
> *At their death they are withered and dry.*

*Therefore the stiff and unbending is the disciple
   of death.
The gentle and yielding is the disciple of life.
(Feng & English)*

Here, gentleness is vitality. Yielding is a kind of strength. This passage suggests that to live well — and to die well — is to remain supple in the face of change. It is to adapt, to release, to be moved by life rather than resist it.

In a world where the ecological crisis constantly reminds us of our limits, the Daoist approach to death offers a crucial corrective to modern hubris. It teaches us to live within our means, to recognize our dependence on the earth, and to understand our place in the great web of life. Death is not just an individual event; it is part of the ecosystem of existence. Our bodies return to the soil. Our stories become part of the cultural memory. Our acts ripple outward long after we are gone.

From this angle, death becomes an act of participation. It is not the negation of life but its culmination. The Way of Kinship calls us to see death not as a wall but as a passage — not as the end of meaning but as its deepest invitation. What will we do with the time we are given? How will we live knowing we will not live forever?

The answers are not found in rigid doctrines or promises of eternal life. They are found in presence. In connection. In the choice to live in harmony with ourselves, with others, and with the world. The Daodejing does not ask us to conquer death. It asks us to understand it, to flow with it, and to let it shape us into wiser, more compassionate beings.

Death, in this view, is not something to fear or defeat. It is something to walk with. To acknowledge. To befriend. And when the time comes, to embrace with a quiet trust that we, too, are part of the ten thousand things returning to the root.

This is the Way of Kinship. This is the gift of being alive.

CONCLUSION

PERCEPTION REVISITED

When I began this book, I suggested that a change in perception changes everything. How we perceive the world shapes our experience of it. And how we experience the world, in turn, shapes how we act in it. Perception is not a passive reception of data — it is the lens through which meaning emerges, relationships are formed, and value is assigned. To shift that lens is to open the possibility of becoming something new.

Throughout these pages, we have explored what it means to see the world through the lens of oneness: a grounded recognition of interdependence, co-creation, and mutual becoming. Oneness, in this sense, is not a metaphysical claim but a perceptual orientation — one that attunes us to the reality that nothing stands alone. Every moment, every being, every choice arises within a web of relations that precede and exceed us.

This way of seeing does not require us to reject individuality or erase distinctions. Instead, it invites us to see how the parts gain meaning only in context — how even the most private emotion is shaped by the surrounding social field; how every decision carries ripples through a wider world; how our well-being is always, in some measure, a collective achievement. It is a vision that offers no easy certainty but much clarity. No grand system but deep alignment. Not a fixed doctrine but an ongoing discipline of presence, humility, and response.

As we've seen, this orientation toward oneness transforms more than thought — it reshapes feeling, behavior, and policy. Inner harmony begins with observing and responding to what arises without grasping. Social harmony is not found through enforced conformity but through resonance, mutuality, and the courageous presence of difference. Environmental harmony does not come from dominating the natural world but from listening deeply to its rhythms and reestablishing ourselves within the broader fabric of life.

Even in moments of rupture (personal or political), oneness offers a path toward restoration. To act wisely is to act with full awareness of connection: that harm to one is harm to many and that healing must begin with understanding the relationships that make healing possible. The Way of Kinship, then, is not an escape from the world. It is an invitation to be more fully embedded in it — to care more honestly, act more carefully, and live more simply in the service of what sustains life.

This is not always easy. The modern world often pulls us in the opposite direction: toward fragmentation, isolation, speed, and control. It encourages a self that is bounded, competitive, and always managing. But there is another way. A way that is quieter, slower, and less certain — but more honest. A way that doesn't seek to master life but to join it more fully. A way that begins by shifting how we see and ends by transforming how we are.

That is the Way of Kinship. It begins not with belief but with attention. Not with answers but with attunement. Not with a demand to fix the world but with an invitation to be with the world — more openly, more wisely, and with a gentler hand.

WE GET TO PARTICIPATE

It is a gift to be alive: raw, wild, fleeting, and precious beyond words. There is no justification for it, no ultimate explanation. We were not owed this life. And yet here we are, conscious for a moment, woven into a vast and mysterious web of existence that far precedes us and will long outlast us.

In this book, we've explored how a shift in perception — toward interdependence, toward harmony, toward kinship with all things — can reshape how we live. We've questioned inherited ideas of selfhood, morality, government, and even death. But under it all runs a quiet, radiant thread: awe. The simple, irreducible astonishment that anything is happening at all and that we get to be part of it.

There is no blueprint for how to be. There is no one coming to hand us the meaning of life. But there is this breath, this moment, this tree, this person, this aching, or this joy. And we can respond with presence. The fact that we get to participate in this unfolding world, to contribute even in small ways to the flow of life, is an unmatched gift.

Participation doesn't require that we fix the world. It asks only that we show up honestly and that we learn to listen, to tend, and to respond with care. The Way of Kinship is not about becoming a perfect version of ourselves or controlling the outcome of events. It's about being in the world as it is and finding within it a rhythm that resonates with our deepest integrity. We only need to begin paying attention to our relationships, to our choices, to the ripples we send out.

Living with this awareness can feel like both a burden and a liberation. On one hand, there's the weight of knowing how much harm can be done when we act without connection. On the other hand, there is the freedom of realizing that we are not isolated fragments but threads in a living tapestry. Nothing we do is separate. No kindness is wasted. No act of care is lost.

We get to participate. We get to shape culture, create beauty, offer compassion, protect the vulnerable, speak truth, learn, adapt, and grow. We get to dance with uncertainty. We get to grieve. We get to love. These are not small things. They are the texture of a meaningful life.

Even our limits, our mortality, give shape to this gift. The knowledge that it all ends one day — that we, too, will fall back into the earth — imbues every choice with significance. If life is short, then how we live matters more, not less. To care, to build, to nurture, to accept — these are sacred gestures in a world that has no promise of permanence.

The Way of Kinship is not a doctrine to be followed; it is a way of being to be practiced. It doesn't hand us certainty. It offers us orientation. It says: the world is whole, even in its brokenness. You are part of that wholeness. Tend to it. Let it tend to you. And above all, stay awake to the reality that you are here, now, and alive.

And that — against all odds, against the vast silence of the cosmos — is enough.

We get to participate. May we do so with courage, humility, and love.

KINSHIP CAFE

The journey does not end with these pages. If the ideas in The Way of Kinship have spoken to you, I invite you to join www.Kinship.Cafe — an online community dedicated to exploring the Daodejing and living its wisdom together.

At Kinship Cafe, you'll find space for thoughtful conversation, a supportive community of fellow travelers, and opportunities to go deeper through:

• Weekly Zoom gatherings where we explore passages of the Daodejing in depth.

• Self-paced courses designed to help you integrate these teachings into your daily life.

• Discussion forums where you can share reflections, ask questions, and connect with others walking the Way.

We are made stronger by diversity. We invite you to share your voice.

WORKS CITED

Addiss, Stephen, and Stanley Lombardo. *Tao Te Ching*. Hackett Publishing Company, 1993.

Breer, Paul. *The Spontaneous Self: Viable Alternatives to Free Will*. Xlibris Corporation, 2012.

Chen, Ellen M. *Tao Te Ching: A New Translation with Commentary*. Paragon House Publishers, April 1998.

Feng, Gia-Fu, and Jane English, with Toinette Lippe. *Tao Te Ching*: With Over 150 Photographs by Jane English. Knopf Doubleday Publishing Group (Vintage), November 1, 2011.

Hinton, David, translator. *Analects*. Counterpoint Press, 2014.

Ivanhoe, Philip J. *The Daodejing of Laozi*. Hackett Publishing Company, August 1, 2003.

Komjathy, Louis. *Daode Jing: A Contextual, Contemplative, and Annotated Bilingual Translation*. Square Inch Press, 2024.

LaFargue, Michael. *Tao and Method: A Reasoned Approach to the Tao Te Ching*. State University of New York Press, August 30, 1994.

McDonald, John H., translator. *Tao Te Ching*. Arcturus Publishing, October 2017.

Pine, Red, translator. *Lao-Tzu's Taoteching: With Selected Commentaries from the Past 2,000 Years*. Copper Canyon Press, 2009.

Rovelli, Carlo. *The Order of Time*. Riverhead Books, 2018.

Wang, Robin R. *Yinyang: The Way of Heaven and Earth in Chinese Thought and Culture*. Cambridge University Press, 2009.

Watson, Burton, translator. *The Complete Works of Zhuangzi*. Columbia University Press, 2013.

FURTHER READING

RECOMMENDED TRANSLATIONS OF THE DAODEJING

Addiss, Stephen, and Stanley Lombardo. *Tao Te Ching*. Hackett Publishing Company, 1993.

Feng, Gia-Fu, and Jane English, with Toinette Lippe. *Tao Te Ching*: With Over 150 Photographs by Jane English. Knopf Doubleday Publishing Group (Vintage), November 1, 2011.

Ivanhoe, Philip J. *The Daodejing of Laozi*. Hackett Publishing Company, August 1, 2003.

ADDITIONAL TRANSLATION OF THE DAODEJING

Ames, Roger T., and David L. Hall. *Dao De Jing: A Philosophical Translation*. Random House Publishing Group, 2003 (paperback); eBook 2010.

Chen, Ellen M. *Tao Te Ching: A New Translation with Commentary*. Paragon House Publishers, April 1998.

Hinton, David. *Tao Te Ching*. Catapult (Counterpoint LLC), 2015.

Komjathy, Louis. *Daode Jing: A Contextual, Contemplative, and Annotated Bilingual Translation*. Square Inch Press, 2024.

Laska, P. J. *The Original Wisdom of the Dao De Jing: A New Translation and Commentary*. ECCS Books, January 2012.

Pine, Red, translator. *Lao-Tzu's Taoteching: With Selected Commentaries from the Past 2,000 Years*. Copper Canyon Press, 2009.

Fisher, Paul. *The Annotated Laozi*. State University of New York Press, 2023.

DAOIST PHILOSOPHY AND HISTORICAL CONTEXT

Allan, Sarah. *The Way of Water and Sprouts of Virtue*. State University of New York Press, January 1, 1997.

Bruya, Brian. *Ziran: The Philosophy of Spontaneous Self-Causation*. State University of New York Press, July 1, 2022.

Coutinho, Steve. *An Introduction to Daoist Philosophies*. Columbia University Press, 2014.

Hansen, Chad. *A Daoist Theory of Chinese Thought: A Philosophical Interpretation*. Oxford University Press, 2000.

Hinton, David. *China Root: Taoism, Ch'an, and Original Zen*. Shambhala Publications, September 29, 2020.

Ivanhoe, Philip J. *Oneness: East Asian Conceptions of Virtue, Happiness, and How We Are All Connected*. Oxford University Press, 2017.

Moeller, Hans-Georg. *The Moral Fool: A Case for Amorality*. Columbia University Press, July 2009.

Moeller, Hans-Georg. *The Philosophy of the Daodejing*. Columbia University Press, 2006.

Needham, Joseph, with Wang Ling. *Science and Civilisation in China, Volume 2: History of Scientific Thought*. Cambridge University Press, 1956.

Valmisa, Mercedes. *Adapting: A Chinese Philosophy of Action*. Oxford University Press, 2021.

Van Norden, Bryan W. *Introduction to Classical Chinese Philosophy*. Hackett Publishing, 2011.

Wang, Robin R. *Yinyang: The Way of Heaven and Earth in Chinese Thought and Culture*. Cambridge University Press, 2009.

Watson, Burton, translator. *The Complete Works of Zhuangzi*. Columbia University Press, 2013.

NATURALISM

Carrier, Richard. *Sense and Goodness without God: A Defense of Metaphysical Naturalism*. AuthorHouse, February 23, 2005.

Clark, Thomas W. *Encountering Naturalism: A Worldview and Its Uses*. Center for Naturalism, March 1, 2007.

Rue, Loyal D. *Nature Is Enough: Religious Naturalism and the Meaning of Life*. State University of New York Press, July 2, 2012.

THE BRAIN AND HUMAN NATURE

Barrett, Lisa Feldman. *How Emotions Are Made: The Secret Life of the Brain*. Houghton Mifflin Harcourt, 2017.

Haidt, Jonathan. *The Happiness Hypothesis: Finding Modern Truth in Ancient Wisdom*. Basic Books, 2006.

May, Todd. *Death* (The Art of Living). Routledge, 2009.

Sapolsky, Robert M. *Behave: The Biology of Humans at Our Best and Worst.* Penguin Press, 2017.

Seth, Anil. *Being You: A New Science of Consciousness.* Faber and Faber, 2021.

REALITY

Carroll, Sean M. *The Big Picture: On the Origins of Life, Meaning, and the Universe Itself.* Dutton, 2016.

Krauss, Lawrence M. *The Greatest Story Ever Told—So Far: Why Are We Here?* Atria Books, March 21. 2017.

Rovelli, Carlo. *Helgoland: Making Sense of the Quantum Revolution.* Riverhead Books, 2021.

_____. *The Order of Time.* Riverhead Books, 2018.

DETERMINISM

Breer, Paul. *The Spontaneous Self: Viable Alternatives to Free Will.* Xlibris Corporation, 2012.

Sapolsky, Robert M. *Determined: A Science of Life Without Free Will.* Penguin Press, 2023.